lonely planet

POCKET

CANBERRA

TOP SIGHTS · LOCAL EXPERIENCES

SAMANTHA FORGE

Contents

Australian Parliament House (p34) viewed from
the Australian War Memorial (p74)
MARK HIGGINS/SHUTTERSTOCK ©

Welcome to Canberra

Lately Canberra has been staking a claim for the title of Australia's coolest city – and we're not just talking winter temperatures. The nation's 'bush capital' has transformed into a cosmopolitan metropolis, with superb dining and world-class cultural experiences right alongside wildlife-filled bushland and serene lakeshore trails. There's plenty to keep visitors entertained, whether you're here for the weekend or have a bit more time to spare.

Civic (p73) from above
MARTIN OLLMAN/500PX ©

Top Sights

National Gallery of Australia

Visit Australia's national art collection. **p40**

Australian Parliament House

The heart of Australian democracy. **p34**

Australian War Memorial

Memorial to Australia's war dead. **p74**

Australian National Botanic Gardens

A microcosm of Australian flora. **p60**

LIZ JARMOW/SHUTTERSTOCK ©

QUESTACON DESIGNED BY LAWRENCE NIELD/GREG BRAVE/SHUTTERSTOCK ©

JEFFSHELTN/SHUTTERSTOCK ©

Questacon

A playful, interactive science museum. **p44**

Canberra Wine Region

Canberra's best-kept secret. **p128**

Tidbinbilla Nature Reserve
Australian fauna in the wild. **p124**

Namadgi National Park
Wilderness on Canberra's doorstep. **p126**

DANIELE/GETTY IMAGES ©

RODRIGO LOUREZIN/SHUTTERSTOCK ©

NATIONAL ARBORETUM DESIGNED BY TONKIN ZULAIKHA GREER ARCHITECTS

National Arboretum
Local and international tree repository. **p70**

Eating

For such a small city, Canberra punches well above its weight on the culinary front, with a sophisticated dining scene catering to politicians and locals alike. Established dining hubs include Civic, Kingston and Manuka. New Acton, the Kingston foreshore development and Lonsdale St in Braddon are the hippest new areas.

Where to Eat When

Canberra's dining scene is very schedule-specific. Mid-week you'll find the most action around the city centre, with a secondary hotspot in Barton, close to Parliament. On the weekends, the focus shifts to the suburbs, with locals flocking to satellite villages such as Kingston, Manuka, Ainslie and Dickson. The exception is Braddon, which attracts the punters all week long.

Best Mod-Oz Restaurants

Terra Innovative modern Australian dining at its most approachable. (p82)

Muse The literary-themed menu makes for good reading and even better eating. (pictured above; p117)

Pilot Spectacular seasonal dishes in Ainslie. (p107)

Otis Playful takes on Australian favourites in Kingston village. (p119)

Best Breakfasts

Cupping Room Interesting, seasonal dishes and truly excellent coffee. (p66)

Morning Glory Traditional breakfast dishes are given an Asian twist at this New Acton cafe. (p66)

Rye A cosy wood-burning fire and Scandi-inspired comfort food give you a real feeling of *hygge*. (p93)

Highroad Dickson locals flock to this light, modern cafe for flavourful breakfasts and smooth espresso. (p104)

Maple & Clove Light, healthy breakfasts here are chock-full of seasonal ingredients. (p55)

Best Asian Dining

Lazy Su A wall of lucky cats invite you to dine on Japanese/Korean fusion with a twist. (p94)

Akiba Stylish pan-Asian restaurant right in the heart of Civic. (p82)

GEORGE FRANCIS DUNFORD/LONELY PLANET ©

Asian Noodle House Locals come from miles around to slurp Canberra's best laksa. (p105)

Wild Duck Superb fine-dining restaurant serving pan-Asian dishes. (p119)

Lilotang Elegant Japanese dining tucked away in Barton's hotel district. (p54)

Best Pizza

Agostini's We can't go past the wood-fired pizzas at this spot in the East Hotel, cooked right before your eyes. (p116)

Mama Dough Your local takeaway pizzeria elevated to a new level in Ainslie. (p105)

Urban Thyme Grab a takeaway *manouche* (Lebanese-style pizza) while wandering the markets. (p123)

Four Winds Winery Wood-fired pizzas make a great lunch stop in nearby Murrumbateman. (p131)

Best Vegan Spots

Au Lac Order fresh, healthy dumplings, stir-fries and other noodle dishes at this vegan cafe. (p106)

Sweet Bones Delicious all-day vegan breakfasts and other baked goods. (p95)

Lazy Su This trendy spot has a full vegan banquet as well as several a la carte dishes. (p94)

Messina Sweet-tooths will be thrilled to know that the sorbet flavours at Messina are all vegan. (p93)

Worth a Trip

You'll need to travel out to the southern suburbs to find Canberra's top-rated restaurant, **Aubergine** (☏ 02-6260 8666; www.aubergine.com.au; 18 Barker St, Griffith; 4-course menu per person $98; ☺ 6-10pm Mon-Sat). The menu is exciting, innovative and seasonally driven. Although only a four-course menu is offered, you can choose between a handful of options for most courses.

Drinking

During the day, most of Canberra's village-like suburban centres are home to at least one excellent cafe perfect for sipping coffee and watching the world go by. In the evenings, though, nightlife tends to be concentrated in Civic and around Lonsdale and Mort Sts in Braddon. New Acton, Kingston and Manuka are also worth a look.

Neighbourhoods

You'll always find somewhere for a drink in Canberra, but it's true the city can be a bit of a ghost town on weeknights, during university holidays and when parliament isn't sitting. Mondays and Tuesdays can be quiet even in the hottest of hotspots, and many venues (including the wineries on Canberra's outskirts) are closed on those days, so plan ahead carefully if you're looking for a big night on the town.

Coffee

It might surprise some visitors to find that Canberra has a coffee scene to rival that of Sydney or Melbourne, including a handful of local roasters churning out their own high-quality beans. The dense concentration of public servants, politicians, journalists, students and other caffeine hounds in Canberra means you're never very far from a really good brew.

Best Pubs

Edgar's Inn Great dining deals and a friendly vibe make this Ainslie spot a hit with locals. (p106)

Old Canberra Inn Canberra's oldest pub is still going strong. (p107)

Public Bar This leafy, spacious pub on the corner in Manuka is a great place for an afternoon beverage or two. (p120)

Dock On the Kingston foreshore, this local favourite caters to all comers. (p120)

Best Wine Bars

Bar Rochford Staff at this classy, European-style wine bar upstairs in Civic really know their stuff. (p84)

Joe's Bar This sophisticated operation at the East Hotel has a great selection of Italian wines. (p119)

GEORGE FRANCIS DUNFORD/LONELY PLANET ©

Canberra Wine House The location is more than a bit bizarre, but the all-local wine list is a winner. (p108)

Best Cocktails

Molly Expert bartenders whip up intriguing cocktails at this atmospheric speakeasy. (p84)

Parlour Wine Room When the sun is out, sip sophisticated drinks on the umbrella-covered deck in New Acton. (p69)

Monster Kitchen & Bar The cocktail list here ranges from the classic to the fantastical, like the quirkily named Sally Finds a Friend. (p66)

Highball Express Highball's Cuban theme means you can't go past the rum-based cocktails. (pictured above; p85)

Best Coffee

Ona Find fabulous filter coffee at this lush cafe on a square in Manuka. (p119)

Cupping Room A separate coffee tasting menu helps you select the perfect kind of bean for your tastes. (p66)

Kyō Coffee Project So hip it hurts, this petite cafe in Braddon serves up perfect batch brew. (p96)

Local Press Down by the Kingston Foreshore you'll find this gem, which does a roaring trade. (p120)

Barrio Collective Coffee Braddonites sit at the tables here supping smooth espresso all day long. (p97)

Highroad A haven of cafe cool in suburban Dickson, grab a flat white and watch the world go past the windows. (p104)

Local Wines

Canberra's wine region (p128) produces high-country cool-climate wines, with riesling and shiraz the star performers. Most of the best wineries are actually just across the border in NSW, north of the city. For further options, visit www.canberrawines.com.au.

Shopping

Canberra's large transient population means it isn't a haven for shopaholics in the same way as its larger metropolitan rivals, but there are still plenty of spots to get a dose of retail therapy.

Market Culture

Canberrans love a farmers market, and the proximity of the surrounding countryside means there is always a plethora of farm-fresh produce available. The big-hitter is the Capital Region Farmers Market (p109) held at Exhibition Park every Saturday, but there are plenty of smaller markets dotted around the suburbs that are definitely worth a wander if you're in town on a weekend.

Best Fashion & Accessories

Lost Vintage Wear your hippest duds to browse the racks at this tiny vintage treasure. (p99)

Kin Gallery Pick up something sparkly from a wide array of local and international jewellery designers. (p98)

Lonsdale St Traders You're sure to find something to your taste at this curated collection of small retailers in Braddon. (p99)

Canberra Centre Every fashion brand under the sun is represented at this large central shopping mall. (p87)

Best Bookshops

National Library Bookshop Pick up titles by Australian authors at this friendly bookshop inside the library. (p57)

Paperchain One of our favourite bookshops in Canberra, this store in Manuka has a fabulous selection. (p121)

Book Lore Rummage among overstuffed shelves at this treasure trove in Lyneham. (p109)

Curatoreum You'll find a great selection of gift books and other titles here. (p69)

TONYNG/SHUTTERSTOCK ©

Best for Souvenirs & Gifts

Curatoreum As curated as its name suggests, this shop is full of exquisitely beautiful things. (p69)

Bison Home This local ceramics designer makes perfectly covetable cups and vases that are great gifts. (p98)

Craft ACT Local makers exhibit and sell their wares at this tiny store and museum space. (p87)

Canberra Glassworks Pick up beautiful glassware by local artists in this heritage building in Kingston. (p121)

Best for Picnic Supplies

Capital Region Farmers Market The very best of local produce is on show at this bustling local market. Plan to eat a big breakfast here. (pictured above; p109)

Fyshwick Fresh Food Markets Delis, grocers, bakeries and more are all clustered together inside the Fyshwick markets. (p121)

Bitten Goodfoods Find a wide array of organic wholefoods at this grocer in Braddon. (p99)

Spending up Big

If you're really looking to hit the plastic hard during your visit, your best bet is a visit to the Canberra Centre (p87). This conglomeration of buildings and malls is home to department stores, supermarkets, food courts, cinemas and every kind of retail outlet under the sun.

Museums

Canberra is a museum-lover's paradise, with several world-class museums and galleries clustered together by the lakeshore in one of Australia's most impressive cultural collections. Once you've visited the big names, though, there are still plenty of smaller places to explore, and a rotating schedule of excellent temporary exhibitions.

World-Class Collections

Move over, Melbourne, Canberra is Australia's true cultural capital, with two world-class museums (the National Gallery and Portrait Gallery) housing between them a wealth of artworks that would rival the collections of many world cities. You'll never see everything, no matter how long you spend wandering the light-filled rooms, as both museums only have a small portion of their mammoth collections on display at any one time. The upside is that you can return again and again and always find something new to see.

Temporary Exhibitions

Canberra's museums and galleries are renowned for their excellent temporary exhibitions, which often showcase huge international names. The smaller museums are just as likely to get in on the action, with places like the National Library and the Canberra Museum often staging must-see events. Head to www.events.act.gov.au to see what's in town during your visit.

Best Museums

National Gallery of Australia A wonderful collection of Indigenous Australian and Torres Strait Islander art is among this gallery's many highlights. (p40)

National Portrait Gallery See significant faces from Australian history up close and personal. (p50)

Questacon You'll have oodles of family-friendly fun at this interactive science museum. (p44)

National Museum of Australia Explore the many stages of Australian history at this in-depth museum. (p64)

PHILLIP MINNIS/SHUTTERSTOCK ©

Australian War Memorial Sobering exhibitions trace the history of Australia's military endeavours. (p74)

Best Less-Visited Museums

National Film & Sound Archive Stages excellent temporary exhibitions on contemporary film and broadcast culture. (p65)

Canberra Museum & Art Gallery Come for Sidney Nolan's *Ned Kelly* paintings and stay for a fascinating series of temporary exhibitions. (p78)

National Capital Exhibition A scale model of the Canberra basin and an excellent short documentary are among the highlights. (p79)

Museum of Australian Democracy Get the behind-the-scenes goss on the Australian government at Old Parliament House. (pictured above; p50)

Worth a Trip

The **Royal Australian Mint** (☎02-6202 6999; www.ramint.gov.au; Denison St, Deakin; ⏰8.30am-5pm Mon-Fri, 10am-4pm Sat & Sun) is Australia's biggest money-making operation. Its gallery showcases the history of Australian coinage; learn about the 1813 'holey dollar' and its enigmatic offspring, the 'dump'. There's also an observation platform where you can see coins being made (on weekdays). Engaging guided tours (30 minutes) about the history of currency in Australia run regularly throughout the day on the hour; call ahead to check times.

For Kids

Canberra is a family-friendly city, with plenty of space to roam and no huge crowds. Kids like Canberra because there's stacks of cool stuff for them to do. Most of the museums and galleries have kids' programs, and many offer dedicated tours and events for little people – check websites for details.

Accommodation

Hotels are generally accommodating to small guests, and most can provide a cot if you ask. Serviced apartments are also a good choice for families.

Transport

Children under five travel free on public transport, while school-age children pay half the adult fare.

Dining

Many restaurants and cafes have children's menus, and kids are generally welcome everywhere. There are great, kid-friendly cafes inside most of Canberra's top sights, and there are also usually plenty of green spaces around for picnicking.

Best Outdoor Activities

National Arboretum
Children will love the tree-themed Pod Playground here; it features cubbies made of giant acorns, swings shaped like nests and banksia pods to climb on. (Pod Playground is pictured above and was designed by Taylor Cullity Lethlean; p70)

Tidbinbilla Nature Reserve
Keep the kids occupied spotting kangaroos, koalas, platypus and many other animals at this open-range park, which also has plenty of picnic and play facilities. (p124)

Australian National Botanic Gardens
There's plenty for kids to see and do at these expansive gardens, from lizard-watching in the rock gardens to a dedicated children's discovery trail. (p60)

GoBoat
The whole family will enjoy exploring Lake Burley Griffin in your own motorised dinghy – picnic table included. (p116)

Manuka Swimming Pool
On hot days, nothing beats a dip at this Manuka gem, which has plenty of facilities for littlies. (p116)

CHAMELEONSEYE/SHUTTERSTOCK ©

Best Indoor Activities

Questacon The ultimate family spot, this excellent science museum has stacks of hands-on activities to keep little minds happy. (p44)

National Gallery of Australia The dedicated play space on the ground floor of the gallery offers changing installations by Australian artists with craft activities and other fun things especially designed for small hands. (p40)

National Museum of Australia Download the museum Kspace app before your visit to take advantage of the Kspace Augmented Reality Trail, which helps kids explore the galleries via a fun interactive adventure game. (p64)

Museum of Australian Democracy Old Parliament House is home to a fun Play Up exhibition just for kids, which includes dress up clothes and a play room. (p50)

Worth a Trip

It's certainly not the biggest in Australia, but Canberra's **National Zoo & Aquarium** (✆02-6287 8400; www.nationalzoo.com.au; 999 Lady Denman Dr, Weston Creek; adult/child $47/26; 🕑9.30am-5pm) is well laid out and animal friendly, with native fauna such as Tasmanian devils and dingoes to keep the kids amused. It also offers various behind-the-scenes experiences where you can help to feed the sharks, lions, tigers and bears, and interact with rhinos and cheetahs. An adventure playground includes life-size models of animals and is great fun for kids. To get here, catch bus 180 or 181 from the Civic bus interchange.

Parks & Outdoors

Canberra isn't known as Australia's 'bush capital' for nothing – no matter where in town you are, you're never very far from your own personal slice of wilderness. The rivers, lakes and mountains surrounding Canberra offer plenty of opportunities for bushwalking, swimming and cycling.

Bushwalking

Canberra has a huge range of bushwalking opportunities. Close to the city, Black Mountain, Mt Ainslie and Mt Majura all offer well-marked trails and the chance to see local flora and fauna. Further afield, Tidbinbilla Nature Reserve, 40km southwest of the city, has walking and bicycle tracks, a eucalypt forest and a platypus habitat. The nearby Namadgi National Park also offers excellent hiking.

Cycling

Canberra's streets are perfect for cycling, and the city has an extensive network of dedicated cycle paths. The visitor centre (p142) is a good source of information, as is Pedal Power ACT (www.pedalpower. org.au).

Swimming

There are inviting waterholes along the Murrumbidgee River corridor; ask at the visitor centre (p142). A handy website, www.theswimguide. org, advises on the best spots to swim (and the current water quality) in and around Lake Burley Griffin.

On a hot summer's day, the best spot for a dip near the city centre is the Manuka Swimming Pool (p116).

Best Walking

Namadgi National Park
From all-day treks to short strolls and everything in between, this national park on Canberra's southern edge is a haven for outdoor enthusiasts. (p126)

Lake Burley Griffin
Canberra's most iconic outdoor feature is ringed by

ALEX CIMBAL/SHUTTERSTOCK ©

28km of walking and cycling tracks – you never know who you might encounter on a lunchtime stroll. (p78)

Tidbinbilla Nature Reserve You'll never have a better chance of encountering Australian wildlife in their natural habitat than on the many trails at Tidbinbilla. (p124)

Black Mountain The well-trafficked Summit Walk is a popular morning stroll for Canberra residents, but there are also plenty of other trails to explore on the mountain's tree-covered slopes. (p64)

Mt Ainslie Find Canberra's best views at the top of Mt Ainslie, via a heart-pumping 4.5km hike up from the back of the Australian War Memorial. (p104)

Best Parks & Gardens

Australian National Botanic Gardens Green thumbs and plant lovers shouldn't miss these diverse and expansive gardens. (p60)

National Arboretum Acres of forest, superb views and interesting artworks make this a great outing. (p70)

Glebe Park A surprising green space amongst the bustle of the city centre. (p80)

Lennox Gardens This petite lakeside park in Yarralumla has lovely views and several interesting sights. (pictured above; p53)

Kangaroo Spotting

Canberra is one of the best cities in Australia for spotting wild kangaroos. Some of the most likely spots include Weston Park on the shores of Lake Burley Griffin north-west of Parliament House, Government House, Mt Ainslie and Namadgi National Park. You're also practically guaranteed to see kangaroos if you visit Tidbinbilla.

Festivals & Events

KATACARIX/SHUTTERSTOCK ©

Canberra's calendar is jam-packed with events year-round, but there is one big-hitter that draws the crowds to town in every Spring: Floriade. If you're planning on attending, be sure to book accommodation way in advance. To find out what's happening during your visit, see www.events.act.gov.au.

Best Festivals & Events

Floriade (www.floriade australia.com; Common-wealth Park; ☉mid-Sep–mid-Oct) This renowned flower festival (pictured above) draws crowds every year to delight in elaborate floral displays, as well as evening events and performances.

Canberra Balloon Spectacular (www. enlightencanberra.com; ☉Mar) Hot-air balloons lift off from the lawns in front of Old Parliament House every morning during this nine-day festival.

Enlighten (www.enlighten canberra.com; ☉Mar) Canberra institutions are bathed in projections and

keep their doors open late, while musical performances and other outdoor events culminate in an explosive fireworks display.

Art, Not Apart (www. artnotapart.com; New Acton; ☉Mar) This contemporary art festival aims to be like no other festival you've ever seen.

Canberra International Music Festival (www. cimf.org.au; ☉Apr or May) Eleven days of classical-music performances in significant Canberra locations and buildings.

National Folk Festival (www.folkfestival.org.au; Exhibition Park; ☉Easter) A huge program of music, entertainment, markets and camping over five days.

National Multicultural Festival (www.multi culturalfestival.com.au; ☉Feb) A celebration of cultural and linguistic diversity, with three days of art, culture and food in the city centre.

Royal Canberra Show (www.canberrashow.org.au; Exhibition Park; ☉late Feb) The country comes to town: pat a lamb, ride the Ferris wheel, eat some fairy floss and soak up the country-show atmosphere.

Summernats (www. summernats.com.au; Exhibition Park; ☉Jan) The city revs up for the nation's biggest festival of street cars.

Alternative Canberra

DAN BRECKWOLDT/SHUTTERSTOCK ©

You've visited all the main sights, strolled around the lake, checked out Floriade and been kangaroo-spotting at Tidbinbilla – now what? Don't worry, there's still plenty for repeat visitors to do in Australia's capital.

Best Lesser-Known Sights

Jerrabomberra Wetlands Cycle or stroll around this unique ecosystem, a haven for migratory birds. (p123)

Drill Hall Gallery Gaze upon rotating exhibitions by Australian artists at this spot on the ANU campus. (p65)

Mt Majura Less-visited Mt Majura has plenty of opportunities for tramping through the undergrowth. (p104)

National Library of Australia Excellent exhibitions display artefacts and ephemera from Australia's past. (p51)

National Carillon Stop by at 12.30pm on Wednesdays and Sundays for a bellringing recital. (pictured above; designed by Cameron, Chisholm & Nicol; p79)

Best Suburban Eats

Pilot First-class dining tucked away at the edge of Ainslie. (p107)

Highroad This slick Dickson cafe wouldn't look out of place in the centre of Melbourne or Sydney. (p104)

Edgar's Inn Locals flock to this friendly pub in the heart of Ainslie. (p106)

Front Part art gallery, part cafe, serving sophisticated fare in Lyneham. (p107)

Local Press You may have to queue for a table at this popular lakeside cafe. (p120)

Worth a Trip

In 1834, when convicts were sent in to clear this land on the edge of Murrumbidgee River for grazing, Tharwa was a wild frontier. Now it's a pretty slice of rural landscape, ringed by hills and with a garden that wouldn't be out of place in the Cotswolds. It's well worth the trip 25km south from Canberra to explore the gracious **Lanyon Homestead** (☎02-6235 5677; www.historicplaces.com.au; Tharwa Dr, Tharwa; adult/child $7/5; ⏰10am-4pm Tue-Sun).

Four Perfect Days

Day 1

CHAMELEONSEYE/SHUTTERSTOCK ©

Start with breakfast at one of the city's excellent cafes – perhaps **Ona** (p119) or **Maple & Clove** (p55) – before making a beeline for the museum quarter to beat the crowds.

Check out the masterpieces at the **National Gallery of Australia** (p40), find familiar faces at the **National Portrait Gallery** (pictured above; p50) or keep the kids entertained at **Questacon** (p44). Lunch at the excellent **Portrait Cafe** (p56) before climbing the hill to **Parliament House** (p34) for a guided tour.

Once you're tired of politics, wander over to nearby Kingston, stopping for a drink at **Ostani** (p57) or **Joe's Bar** (p119). Dine either in Kingston village or on the foreshore – try **Morks** (p117) or **Otis** (p119).

Day 2

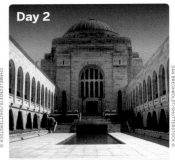

DAN BRECKWOLDT/SHUTTERSTOCK ©

On the second day, breakfast in Acton at the **Cupping Room** (p66) or **Močan & Green Grout** (p67), then wander through the leafy ANU campus to the **Australian National Botanic Gardens** (p60) in time for the 11am guided tour.

Head over to trendy Braddon for a spot of window-shopping, lunching at **Rye** (p93) or **Lazy Su** (p94). Then spend the afternoon at the **Australian War Memorial** (pictured above; p74), staying for the 5pm Last Post Ceremony.

Dine at one of Civic's numerous restaurants – **Terra** (p82) or **Akiba** (p82) – before barhopping between some of the city's best bars; be sure to hit **Molly** (p84) and **Bar Rochford** (p84) before dancing the night away at **88mph** (p68).

Day 3

STEVEN TRITTON/SHUTTERSTOCK ©

Day 4

WORAWOOT TONG/SHUTTERSTOCK ©

On day three, start with breakfast at **Highroad** (pictured above; p104) on your way out into the countryside, either visiting the native animals at **Tidbinbilla Nature Reserve** (p124) or strapping on your hiking shoes for a bushwalk in **Namadgi National Park** (p126). Don't forget to pack a picnic for lunch.

On your way back, stop off at the charming **Lanyon Homestead** (p23) before calling ahead to reserve a table at **Agostini's** (p116) or **Lilotang** (p54). If you still have some go left, check out the nightlife in Kingston or Manuka, maybe taking in a film at **Capitol Cinemas** (p121).

On day four, head out to sleepy Hall for breakfast at **Kynefin** (p111) before checking out the town's historic buildings.

Once it's a more reasonable hour, visit some of the region's excellent local wineries, stopping in at **Eden Road** (p129), **Clonakilla** (p129) and **Brindabella** (p131). Lunch on wood-fired pizza at **Four Winds** (p131).

Spend your last afternoon soaking up the atmosphere strolling around **Lake Burley Griffin** (pictured above; p78), before heading to New Acton for dinner, dining at **Monster Kitchen & Bar** (p66). End your trip with drinks on the balcony at **Parlour Wine Room** (p69) before descending in the elevator to **Black Market Bar** (p68) for a final cocktail.

Need to Know

For detailed information, see Survival Guide p133

Currency
Australian Dollar ($)

Language
English

Visas
All visitors to Australia need a visa, except New Zealanders.

Money
ATMs are easy to find and most accept international cards. Most businesses – even, increasingly, market-stall holders – accept payment by card.

Time
Australian Eastern Standard/Daylight Saving Time (GMT plus 10/11 hours)

Tipping
Tipping is rarely necessary, though some high-end places will add a 10% to 15% service charge to your bill. Many bars and cafes have a 'tip jar' for loose change.

Daily Budget

Budget: Less than $150
Dorm bed: $35–45
Daily bus ticket: $9.60
Takeaways meals: $15–25
Happy-hour drink: $7
Entry to permanent exhibits in museums: free

Midrange: $150–350
Double room in midrange hotel: $150–200
Speciality coffee: $5–8
Lunch at a cafe: $25–35
Two-course dinner: $60
Glass of wine: $12–15
Entry to temporary exhibitions: $15–25

Top end: More than $350
Double room in fancy hotel: $250-plus
Taxi from airport: $30
Four-course tasting menu: $80–120
Hot-air-balloon ride: $330
Winery tour: $200

Advance Planning

Two months before Book hotel rooms to get the best rate (or even earlier if visiting during parliamentary sitting weeks or Floriade).

One month Make dinner reservations at popular restaurants.

One week before Check online to see what temporary exhibitions are taking place during your stay; book tickets in advance.

Arriving in Canberra

✈ Canberra Airport

Buses run regularly from the airport (pictured below) into the city between 6am and 6pm (adult/child $5/2.50, 20 to 40 minutes); a taxi to the centre should be around $30.

🚌 Jolimont Centre

Long-distance coaches arrive at this city-centre terminal. It is within easy walking distance of several bus stops and the light-rail line.

🚌 Canberra Railway Station

Regular buses connect the railway station with the city centre (15 minutes) and other destinations around Canberra.

Getting Around

🚲 Bicycle

Canberra has an extensive network of on-road bicycle lanes and off-road cycling routes, making two wheels an excellent option for getting around the city.

🚌 Bus

The bus network, operated by Transport Canberra (📞 13 17 10; www.transport.act.gov.au; single adult/child $5/2.50, day pass $9.60/4.80), will get you to most places of interest in the city.

🚗 Car

Canberra's wide and relatively uncluttered streets make driving easy, even during so-called 'peak hour'.

🚋 Light Rail

Canberra's new light-rail line runs from Civic to Gungahlin via Dickson.

Canberra Neighbourhoods

Dickson & the North (p101)
Stretching out into bushland on every side, Canberra's leafy northern suburbs have plenty of self-contained village centres to explore.

National Arboretum
👁

Australian National Botanic Gardens
👁

Acton (p59)
Students from the nearby Australian National University bring a youthful exuberance to this developing pocket of urban cool.

Parliament, Parkes & Barton (p33)
Canberra's lakeside cultural quarter is home to Parliament House and several world-class museums.

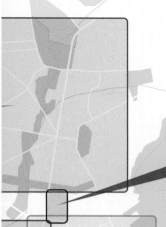

Braddon (p91)
This old industrial area is quickly becoming Canberra's hottest suburb, with more baristas per square metre than anywhere else in town.

Civic (p73)
The city's central business district offers more than its fair share of excellent places to drink and dine.

Australian War Memorial

Questacon

National Gallery of Australia 👁

Australian Parliament House 👁

Kingston & Manuka (p113)
These busy village centres are packed with locals on weekends, when you can cafe-hop all the way to the newly developed foreshore.

Explore
Canberra

View over Canberra LEELAKAJONKIJ/GETTY IMAGES ©

Explore ✦

Parliament, Parkes & Barton

In Canberra, all roads don't lead to Rome but to Capital Hill, atop of which sits the imposing Parliament House. Surrounding the hill, in ever increasing circles, are the suburbs of Parkes, Barton and Yarralumla, whose wide and leafy avenues are home to a variety of government buildings. The lakeside is also host to many of the city's top sights, including the National Gallery of Australia, National Portrait Gallery and Questacon.

The Short List

○ **Australian Parliament House (p34)** Strolling the corridors of power and watching Parliament in action.

○ **National Gallery of Australia (p40)** Admiring world-class artworks and temporary exhibitions.

○ **Questacon (p44)** Touching, poking, jumping on, leaping over and falling into the interactive exhibits.

○ **National Portrait Gallery (p50)** Meeting old and new Australian faces at this national treasure trove.

○ **Museum of Australian Democracy (p50)** Learning about the origins of the Australian parliamentary system.

Getting There & Around

🚌 Parkes, Barton and Capital Hill are easily accessed by buses from all across the city.

🚗 Parking is available near all the main sights, including at Parliament House, the National Gallery and Questacon (weekdays per hour $2.50, weekends free).

Neighbourhood Map on p48

Australian Parliament House (p34) TARAS VYSHNYA/SHUTTERSTOCK ©

Top Sight 📷
Australian Parliament House

Built in 1988, Australia's national parliament building is a graceful and deeply symbolic piece of architecture. Sitting atop Capital Hill, the building is crossed by two axis, north–south and east–west, representing the historical progression and legislative progression of Australian democracy. There's plenty to see inside, whether the politicians are haranguing each other in the chambers or not.

◉ MAP P48, C5

☑ 02-6277 5399

www.aph.gov.au

Parliament Dr

admission free

🕘 9am-5pm

Forecourt Mosaic

Approaching via the public entrance at the top of Federation Mall, the first significant element visitors encounter is the 196-sq-metre mosaic *Possum and Wallaby Dreaming* (1986–87; pictured left), based on the artwork of the same name by Warlpiri artist Michael Nelson Jagamara. It sits in the centre of a ceremonial pool, symbolising the island continent of Australia. The mosaic is constructed from over 90,000 individually cut pieces of granite, which were carefully selected to match the colours in the original painting. The work symbolises the spiritual connection between Aboriginal and Torres Strait Islander people and their land. The original artwork is part of the Parliament House collection and is sometimes on display in the corridors.

Marble Foyer

After passing through security, visitors arrive in the imposing marble foyer, with 48 marble columns soaring the entire height of the building. The marble here was imported from Europe – the pink Atlantide Rosa marble from Portugal, the green Cipollino marble from Italy and the Paradise white marble from Belgium – to represent European arrival in Australia. On the floor, the black Granitello Nero limestone, also from Belgium, is dotted with fossils of sea life that lived some 345 million years ago and is representative of the significance of the ocean to the Australian continent.

From the foyer, two huge marble staircases stretch up to the 2nd floor, where the public galleries begin.

Great Hall

Upon ascending the staircase, visitors first reach the Great Hall, which is used partly for ceremonial national events but is also available

★ Top Tips

o Free 40-minute guided tours depart daily from the desk in the foyer at 9.30am, 11am, 1pm, 2pm and 3.30pm. Arrive 20 minutes in advance to secure your place.

o On nonsitting days, you can also take a 'behind the scenes' tour (adult/child $25/20) of areas not usually open to the public. Book at the desk in the foyer or by calling ☎02 6277 5050.

o From Friday to Sunday, treat yourself to high tea at the Queen's Terrace Cafe (noon to 4pm, per person $35).

✗ Take a Break

You'll spot everyone from political staffers to journos to the pollies themselves at the excellent Queen's Terrace Cafe (p55) on the 1st floor above the main foyer. A range of fresh, well-prepared meals are on offer, as well as cakes and coffee (or wine!).

for public use for everything from weddings to ping-pong tournaments.

At the far end of the hall is the massive 20m wide by 9m high *Great Hall Tapestry,* based on the 1984 artwork *Untitled (Shoalhaven Landscape)* by Arthur Boyd. The artwork depicts a eucalypt forest, the colours blending together in an almost abstract way to give an impression of the movement and texture of the Australian bush. The tapestry took a team of 14 weavers from the Australian Tapestry Workshop almost two years to make, and is one of the largest tapestries in the world. While the tapestry was being made, Halley's Comet appeared in the sky – an incident that was also captured on the famous Bayeux Tapestry – and it was worked into the design (spot it at the top near the centre left).

Historic Memorials Collection

Founded in 1911 by then Prime Minister Andrew Fisher, the Historic Memorials Collection commissions portraits of significant members of the government – most often the head of state, governors-general, prime ministers, presidents of the senate and speakers of the house of representatives, though other portraits, such as the one of Senator Neville Bonner, the first Indigenous Australian member of parliament, have also been commissioned.

At the heart of the collection – and of most interest to visitors – are the portraits of past prime ministers, displayed in mostly chronological order in the Members' Hall. At the time of writing, the most recent acquisition to this collection was a

Chamber of the House of Representatives

Parliament in Action

On sitting days, visitors are free to watch parliamentary proceedings from the public galleries in both houses – you'll need to divest yourself of all belongings at the cloak desk in the Members' Hall first. You'll need a ticket to view Question Time in the House of Representatives (2pm on sitting days); tickets are free, but you must book through the office of the Serjeant-at-Arms (📞 02 6277 4889) before 12.30pm on the day in question. See the website for a calendar of sitting days.

portrait of former Prime Minister Julia Gillard, Australia's first female prime minister, painted by Vincent Fantauzzo (2018). The painters are having trouble keeping up with Australia's current habit of turfing out old prime ministers and installing new ones every few years, it seems – there have been four PMs since Gillard.

Members' Hall

The Members' Hall sits at the centre of Parliament House, at the intersection of both the chronological axis (the hall represents 'the present') and the legislative axis of the building. On the hall's east and west sides, corridors lead to the chambers of the Senate and the House of Representatives.

At the centre of the hall is a large square infinity pool, representing the idea that no one person can stand at the centre of Australian democracy. The pool is made from a single 3.5-sq-metre piece of South Australian black granite, which weighs around eight tonnes. The trickling of the water over the fountain is designed to muffle the sound of conversation, allowing the parliamentarians who congregate on the 1st floor, under the watchful eye of the public gallery, to speak freely without risk of being overheard.

Fountain Failures

The fountain in the Members' Hall is beautiful and practical, but it's not particularly safe. Set flush into the floor, the fountain has proved a hazard for so many politicians and visitors over the years that a special glass barrier is installed around it during special events (like galas at the adjacent Great Hall) to prevent the unwary from going for an unplanned dip.

House of Representatives

The eastern wing of the building is home to the House of Representatives, the lower house of the Australian Parliament, which has 150 members. In homage to Britain's House of Commons, the fittings in the room are green, however shades were specifically selected to reflect the Australian landscape, with varying hues of deep eucalyptus green used throughout the chamber.

Senate

The western wing of Parliament is home to the Senate, Australia's upper house of parliament, with 76 senators – 12 from each state and two from each territory.

Like in the House of Reps, the red colour of the Senate is a homage to the colours used in Britain's upper house (the House of Lords), but in shades reflective of the Australian environment: in this case, the ochre red of the earth, desert blossoms and Uluru.

Rooftop

Lifts head up to the roof. It used to be possible to walk on the lawns up here – a reminder to the politicians below that this is the 'people's house' – but since 2017 a 2.5m-high metal fence has prevented this due to security concerns. As the focal point of Canberra, however, this terrace is still the best place to get a perspective on Walter Burley Griffin's city design. Your eyes are drawn immediately along three axes, with the Australian War Memorial (p74) backed by Mt Ainslie (p104) directly ahead, the commercial centre on an angle to the left and Duntroon (representing the military) on an angle to the right. Interestingly, the church is denied a prominent place in this very 20th-century design.

Revolving-Door Politics

After decades of seemingly stable governments and democratic transitions of power, the two major

Flying the Flag

The flagpole atop Parliament House is one of the largest steel structures in the world; it is 81m tall and weighs 220 tons. The flag that flies on it is impressive too – 12.8m long and 6.4m high, it weighs 22kg.

parties – the centre-left Australian Labor Party (ALP) and the centre-right Coalition of the Liberal and National Parties – have destabilised with a politics of the revolving door (perhaps not helped by the 24-hour news cycle scrutinising politicians' every move). Since 2010, the prime minster of Australia has changed six times and it looks like the soap opera is set to continue...

The Rise of Populism?

There are signs that disaffection with mainstream politics is growing globally and Australia is no exception. Independent politicians are an increasingly powerful force in Australian parliaments. One Nation leader Pauline Hanson returned to the fore with proposals like capping immigration from 'Muslim countries' and compulsory DNA tests for Indigenous people to 'prove their ancestry'. Other signs populism has infected the political discourse in Australia include the parliamentary declaration that 'It's okay to be white', and the copy-and-paste populist slogans plastered on billboards calling for the people to 'Make Australia Great Again'.

Top Sight 📷
National Gallery of Australia

This Australian national art collection is show-cased in an impressive purpose-built gallery within the parliamentary precinct. Almost every big name from Australian and international art, past and present, is represented. Famous works include one of Monet's Waterlilies, several of Sidney Nolan's Ned Kelly paintings, Salvador Dali's Lobster Telephone, an Andy Warhol Elvis print and a triptych by Francis Bacon.

◎ MAP P48, G3

📞 02-6240 6502

www.nga.gov.au

Parkes Pl, Parkes

temporary exhibition prices vary

🕐 10am–5pm

Skyspace

On the museum's south lawn, to the right as you approach the main entrance, you'll spot James Turrell's mammoth Skyspace *Within Without* (2010; pictured left). This interactive artwork is an immersive architectural experience: part water feature, part sculpture, part meditation. Descend under the grassy knoll, past the cloud-reflecting moat, to emerge into an underground cavern whose contrasting colours of aqua and rust are reminiscent of both Australia's red centre and its azure coast. At the centre of the spiralling path you'll find the viewing room – a completely white, domed space with a circular window open to the sky at its zenith. The colours of the room shift depending on the time of day you visit: come near sunrise or sunset for the most arresting display. The sculpture is open 24 hours a day, meaning you can pop by multiple times during your visit and see how the changing weather and light completely alters your perception of the work.

The Aboriginal Memorial

To your right as you enter the main door, *The Aboriginal Memorial* is a large installation of 200 ceremonial hollow log coffins painted by 43 artists from Ramingining in central Arnhem Land. The work was originally conceived by Djon Mundine OAM and its completion was funded by the NGA in 1987. It was created to coincide with the 200-year anniversary of the arrival of the First Fleet to Australia in 1788, and it commemorates the Indigenous Australians who died as a result of European settlement.

A winding pathway, representing the Glyde River in central Arnhem Land, invites you to walk among the painted coffins. The work is intended both as an artistic and political statement, and was seen by Mundine as a kind of war cemetery for those Indigenous Australians who were denied proper burial rites during the brutality of settlement.

★ Top Tips

o Free guided tours depart hourly from 10.30am to 2.30pm from the ground-level foyer.

o A fabulous 'Art Play' area on the ground level is perfect for keeping kids entertained.

o Ditch your backpack in the ground-floor cloakroom (free) to leave you unencumbered while wandering the galleries.

o Parking in the gallery's underground car park is free on weekends and public holidays.

✗ Take a Break

To combat museum fatigue, head to the **NGA Café** (www.nga.gov.au; dishes $10-18; ⏱10am-4pm; 🅿 ❄ 🛜) on the lower-ground floor for well-prepared, cafeteria-style food – including sandwiches, pies and quiches – as well as cakes, coffee and a short wine list.

Australian Art

On the 1st floor, the galleries devoted to showcasing Australian art present an ever-changing display devoted to exploring different facets of what it means to be Australian. Rather than present a simple chronological exhibition, the galleries combine works from across the collection in different mediums – including painting, sculpture, photography and drawing – to highlight key moments and images of national identity. On our most recent visit, one gallery was dedicated to 'Earth and Sky', with various contemporary and historical works exploring how Australian artists have represented the link between the two.

Blue Poles

One of the most well-known works in the gallery's collection is Jackson Pollock's *Blue Poles* (1952), which caused a furore when it was acquired in 1973 as its price – $1.3 million – was the highest ever paid for a contemporary American artwork at the time. The purchase, approved by then Prime Minister Gough Whitlam, was seen by some to epitomise the financial irresponsibility of the Whitlam government. Others – especially in retrospect, as the work has grown in both artistic and financial estimations – saw it as evidence of Whitlam's vision and commitment to the arts.

The work itself is mammoth, over 2m high and almost 5m wide, and is a superlative example of Pollock's abstract expressionist style.

Fog Sculpture

In the sculpture garden, Fujiko Nakaya's *Foggy wake in a desert: An ecosphere* (1982) creates a fine mist that hovers around the garden between 12.30pm and 2pm every day – a fascinating experience.

Yayoi Kusama

One of the gallery's most talked about recent acquisitions is Japanese artist Yayoi Kusama's *Spirit of the Pumpkins Descended into the Heavens* (2015), which opened on the 2nd floor in late 2018. Part of Kusama's ongoing exploration of the concept of 'infinity rooms', the installation consists of a mirrored cube sitting within a yellow-and-black polka-dotted space – inside the cube further mirrors are deployed to give the illusion of a mass of polka-dot pumpkins extending out into infinite space. The work is both playful and thought-provoking; try to visit during a quieter period, when there are less people in the room, to experience its full impact.

Temporary Exhibitions

The gallery is renowned for hosting world-class temporary exhibitions, borrowing works from around the globe. These hugely popular exhibitions can be packed, especially on weekends; if there's a big-name show in town, try to time your visit for a weekday morning. Check online to see what will be on display during your visit.

Top Sight 📷

Questacon

A must-see for anyone travelling with kids, Canberra's science museum has stacks of fun interactive exhibits that feel nothing like what you learned in the classroom. From earthquake simulators to an enormous model of the moon, there's plenty to keep even adults entertained.

👁 **MAP P48, E2**

📞 02-6270 2800

www.questacon.edu.au

King Edward Tce, Parkes

adult/child $23/17.50

🕐 9am-5pm

Colour & Science

Psychedelic Gallery 1 is all about colour. Find out about fluorescence in an aquarium of tropical fish and explore the properties of quantum colour via colour-changing nanoparticles. A digital exhibit shows you how to mix coloured light through pixels, while another lets you test for various kinds of colour-blindness by measuring your sensitivity to red or green light.

Gallery 2 explores the fundamentals of science through interactive exhibits that allow you to explore concepts of force, light and momentum. Play a harp made of light, learn about fluid viscosity, use a bubble projector to make rainbow patterns and fool around with *Recollections Six*, an artwork by Ed Tannenbaum that records the light reflecting around your body and projects your silhouette onto a screen.

Earth & Movement

In Gallery 3, learn about clouds and how we can detect cosmic radiation from the Big Bang, jump as high as you can and measure your own impact on a seismometer, see a tornado develop, watch a display of 'caged lightning' and experience a simulated earthquake in the Earthquake Lab.

The most adrenaline-charged section of the museum, Gallery 7 is home to a wide range of hands-on activities – take your breath away on the 6m free-fall slide, or challenge a robot to a game of air hockey. This is one of the most popular rooms at Questacon, so try to come outside school hours, or early on weekends.

The Moon

At the bottom of the spiral staircase, enter the doorway into the centre of the atrium to find... the moon? Okay, it's not the actual moon, but it's a very good replica, based on high-resolution photographs taken from NASA's Luna Reconnaissance Orbiter mission.

★ Top Tips

o Time your visit to catch one of the regular science shows at the on-site theatre (included in the ticket price). Shows generally take place at 11am, 12pm, 1.30pm and 2.30pm, but check online for updated times before your visit.

o Questacon is popular with school groups visiting Canberra; try to avoid peak school times if you can.

o The Shed in Gallery 5 is a space for tinkering and hands-on activities, including facilitated workshops and activities for kids aged 10 to 110 years.

✖ Take a Break

Refuel at the **Questacon Café** (dishes $10-17; ⊘9am-5pm) with sandwiches, hot chips and other basic but tasty cafe-style fare.

Walking Tour 🥾

Exploring Yarralumla's Embassies

Leafy Yarralumla is Canberra's diplomatic quarter. Hidden among normal suburban streets you'll find nearly 80 embassies housing diplomats from all around the world. A wander around these sedate streets gives a fascinating glimpse into the international flavour of Australia's capital.

Walk Facts
Start Doubleshot
End Lennox Gardens
Length 4.5km; two hours

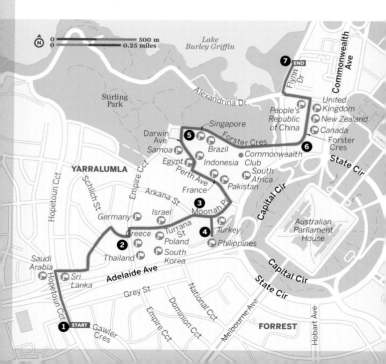

❶ Doubleshot

Before you begin, fortify yourself with a flat white at **Doubleshot** (7 Hopetoun Circuit, Deakin; mains $11-24; ⏱ 6.30am-5pm Mon-Fri, 7am-4pm Sat & Sun), a local hotspot that's renowned for its superlative coffee and fresh, on-trend breakfasts. Once you're caffeinated, stroll down Hopetoun Circuit until you can see the green dome of the Embassy of Saudi Arabia on your left, and the white-columned Sri Lanka High Commission on your right.

❷ Embassy of Japan

Turning right up Hampton Circuit, and heading uphill along Irwin St and Schlich St, you'll reach the manicured lawns of the **Embassy of Japan** (112 Empire Circuit). The white walls and black beams of the elegant embassy buildings are reminiscent of traditional Japanese design. There are several architecturally interesting embassies to view along here, including the South Korean, Thai and Greek embassies.

❸ United States Embassy

Back north along Empire Circuit, you'll turn right past the black-, yellow- and red-accented Embassy of Germany, continuing up the hill past the embassies of Israel and Poland, til you reach the Georgian-style buildings of the **United States Embassy** (Moonah Pl).

❹ High Commission of India

Detour down the hill towards the elegant, symmetrical **High Commission of India** (3-5 Moonah Pl), whose design is clearly influenced by classical Mughal and Hindu architecture. Nearby you'll also spot the embassies of the Philippines and Turkey.

❺ Embassy of Finland

Continuing to skirt the US embassy, veer left onto Perth Ave past the embassies of South Africa, Pakistan and France. Turn right onto Darwin Ave, continuing down the hill past the embassies of Egypt, Indonesia and Samoa, pausing on the corner to admire the sleek glass-and-steel 'Ilmarinen' building of the Embassy of Finland.

❻ High Commission of Papua New Guinea

Turning right onto Forster Cres you'll pass the High Commission of Singapore and the Embassy of Brazil, as well as the exclusive Commonwealth Club. Following the road under Flynn Dr you will come across the stunning **High Commission of Papua New Guinea** (39-41 Forster Cres), with its wonderfully painted roofs and totem poles.

❼ Lennox Gardens

Continuing down towards Coronation Dr, past the Canadian and New Zealand and British embassies, you can't miss the brightly coloured rooftops of the Embassy of the People's Republic of China. End your walk in the lovely Lennox Gardens (p53) on the shore of Lake Burley Griffin.

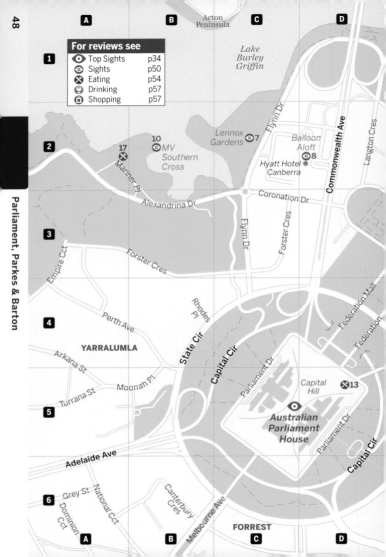

For reviews see

◉	Top Sights	p34
◉	Sights	p50
✖	Eating	p54
🍷	Drinking	p57
🛍	Shopping	p57

Acton Peninsula

Lake Burley Griffin

10 ◉ MV Southern Cross

17 ✖ Mariner Pl

Lennox Gardens ◉ **7**

Flynn Dr

Balloon Aloft ◉ **8**

Hyatt Hotel Canberra

Langton Cres

Commonwealth Ave

Alexandrina Dr

Coronation Dr

Flynn Dr

Forster Cres

Empire Cct

Forster Cres

Rhodes Pl

Perth Ave

State Cir

YARRALUMLA

Arkana St

Turrana St

Moonah Pl

Capital Cir

Parliament Dr

Capital Cir

Capital Hill

✖ **13**

◉ Australian Parliament House

Parliament Dr

Parliament Dr

Adelaide Ave

Grey St

National Cct

Dominion Cct

Canterbury Cres

Melbourne Ave

FORREST

E

F

G

H

1

2

3

4

5

6

500 m
0.25 miles

Central Basin

National Library of Australia
4

Commonwealth Pl

Parkes Pl

Lake Burley Griffin Cruises
9

Reconciliation Place
6

Questacon

National Portrait Gallery
1

5 *High Court of Australia*

Parkes Pl

King Edward Tce

Parkes Pl

PARKES

3 *Aboriginal Tent Embassy*

King George Tce

21 *National Gallery of Australia*

2
Museum of Australian Democracy

Parkes Pl

Queen Victoria Tce

Dorothy Tangney Pl

Mall

Kings Ave

National Cct

Macquarie St

Blackall St

Broughton St
15

16
18

BARTON

Blackall St

Macquarie St

Brisbane Ave

East Basin

Bowen Dr

Bowen Park

State Cir

19

Sydney Ave

National Cct

Bourke St
20
12

11

14

Burbury Cl

Darling St

Macquarie St

Young St

Wentworth Ave

Telopea Park W

Sights

National Portrait Gallery

GALLERY

1 ◉ MAP P48, F2

Occupying a flash, purpose-built building, this wonderful gallery tells the story of Australia through its faces – from wax cameos of Indigenous Australians to colonial portraits of the nation's founding families, to Howard Arkley's Day-Glo portrait of musician Nick Cave. Only around 10% of the collection of more than 3500 works is on display at any one time, so there's always something different to see. New portraits of contemporary Australian figures are also commissioned every year.

There is a good cafe (p56) for post-exhibition coffee and reflection. (☎02-6102 7000; www.portrait. gov.au; King Edward Tce, Parkes; admission free; ☺10am-5pm)

Museum of Australian Democracy

MUSEUM

2 ◉ MAP P48, E3

The seat of government from 1927 to 1988, this elegantly proportioned building offers visitors a taste of the political past. Displays cover Australian prime ministers, the roots of democracy and the history of local protest movements. You can also visit the old Senate and House of Representative chambers, the parliamentary library and the prime minister's office.

Museum of Australian Democracy

LITTLEPANDA29/SHUTTERSTOCK ©

Visiting Parkes

Most of Canberra's big-hitter sights are clustered in Parkes near the lakeshore. At the top of Capital Hill, Parliament House (p34) is visible from kilometres around.

As you descend towards the lake you reach the museum quarter, where the National Gallery of Australia (p40), the National Portrait Gallery and Questacon (p44) can all be found lined up in a row. If you're only in Canberra for a few days, you'll likely spend most of your time here.

Kids will love the Play Up area including dress ups and a play room based on the UN's Right to Shelter, while those with a thing for bling will enjoy the replica crown jewels. (MoAD; 📞02-6270 8222; www.moadoph.gov.au; Old Parliament House, 18 King George Tce, Parkes; adult/child/family $2/1/5; ⏰9am-5pm)

Aboriginal Tent Embassy
HISTORIC SITE

3 👁 MAP P48, E3

First erected in 1972 as a protest against the government's approach to Indigenous land rights, this camp on the lawn in front of Old Parliament House came and went over the subsequent two decades before being re-established in 1992. It has been a constant presence since then, providing a continuing reminder of Indigenous dispossession for those visiting the symbolic heart of Australian democracy. (King George Tce, Parkes)

National Library of Australia
LIBRARY

4 👁 MAP P48, E1

This institution has accumulated more than 10 million items since being established in 1901 and has digitised more than nine billion files. You can pop by the **Main Reading Room** at any time to browse newspapers and magazines by the large windows. Don't miss the **Treasures Gallery**, where artefacts such as Captain Cook's *Endeavour* journal and Captain Bligh's list of mutineers are among the regularly refreshed displays; free 30-minute tours of the gallery are held at 11.30am daily. (📞02-6262 1111; www.nla.gov.au; Parkes Pl, Parkes; admission free; ⏰10am-8pm Mon-Thu, to 5pm Fri & Sat, 1.30-5pm Sun, galleries 10am-5pm daily)

High Court of Australia
NOTABLE BUILDING

5 👁 MAP P48, G2

The glass-and-concrete High Court building sits on the plaza between

Humorists of the House

To look at them, Australia's politicians seem a respectable enough bunch, but a close examination of the parliamentary debating record tells a different tale. There it says the Senate is made up of 'unrepresentative swill', the opposition are a pack of 'dullards', 'mugs' and 'scumbags', while the government are a 'conga line of suck-holes'.

Australia inherited its system of government from England, and along with it the daily spectacle known as Question Time. The idea is that the members ask questions of one another, illuminating for both the press gallery and the public the policies of the day. But a good day is when the political jousting switches to vaudeville and insults fly, roars of indignation rise up from the opposite benches, and suddenly the house is on fire.

Conservative Peter Costello (treasurer 1996–2007) addressed his colleagues thus: 'Let me remind the very voluble Leader of the Opposition, "The Skipper", and his crew on Gilligan's Island over there...'

But the undisputed king of the one-liner was Paul Keating (Labor prime minister 1991–96). 'Howard will wear his leadership like a crown of thorns, and in the parliament I'll do everything to crucify him', he warned his opposite number, John Howard (who eventually beat Keating to become prime minister himself in 1996). Keating welcomed Howard to the parliament with 'Come in, sucker', and accused him of slithering 'out of the Cabinet room like a mangy maggot'.

Howard's predecessors did even worse, with Keating calling one 'a gutless spiv', while declaring that debating another was 'like being flogged with a warm lettuce'.

While those on the other side of politics may prefer to find him entirely unfunny, Keating's lines were so legendary that they became the basis for a successful stage show, *Keating! The Musical*.

the capital's two main art galleries, and, not to be outdone, is home to a large collection of art of its own (pick up a handout inside). It's definitely worth a peek. There's also a small display on the history of the Australian judicial system, and visitors are welcome to view court proceedings when in session.

The High Court sits for two weeks of every month except January and July, with the usual sitting hours from 10.15am to 12.45pm and 2.15pm to 4.15pm daily. Check the schedule online before your visit. (www.hcourt.gov.au; Parkes Pl, Parkes; admission free; ⏰9.45am-4.30pm Mon-Fri, noon-4pm Sun)

Reconciliation Place   PARK

6 ⊙ MAP P48, F2

A section of the grassy public space between Parliament and Lake Burley Griffin has been designated to represent the nation's commitment to the cause of reconciliation between Indigenous and non-Indigenous Australians. It's an unassuming design, with 17 sculptures positioned along the pathways, exploring various aspects of the reconciliation process.

Lennox Gardens   PARK

7 ⊙ MAP P48, C2

These perfectly picnickable gardens on the shore of Lake Burley Griffin are home to a couple of lovely small sights, including the Canberra Nara Peace Park and the Beijing Garden, both worth a wander if you're passing by. (Flynn Dr)

Balloon Aloft   BALLOONING

8 ⊙ MAP P48, D2

Meet in the foyer of the Hyatt for an early-morning flight over Canberra – the ideal way to understand the city's unique design. (📞 02-6249 8660; www.balloonaloft canberra.com.au; 120 Commonwealth Ave, Yarralumla; adult/child from $330/240)

Lake Burley Griffin Cruises   CRUISE

9 ⊙ MAP P48, F2

Informative one-hour lake cruises depart from the wharf in front of the International Flag Display. (📞 0419 418 846; www.lakecruises.

Fire and Water by Judy Watson, Reconciliation Place

LINDA_K/SHUTTERSTOCK ©

com.au; Queen Elizabeth Tce, Parkes; adult/child $20/9; ⏰mid-Sep–May)

MV Southern Cross CRUISE

10 ◉ MAP P48, B2

Offers sightseeing cruises on the lake, with three different pick-up and drop-off locations. Lunch or dinner cruises (adult/child $79/30) are also available. (☎02-6273 1784; www.mvsoutherncross.com.au; 1 Mariner Pl, Yarralumla; adult/child from $20/10)

Eating

Lilotang JAPANESE $$$

11 ✖ MAP P48, F6

Artfully strung rope distracts from an industrial-looking ceiling at this upmarket Japanese restaurant in the Burbury Hotel. Highlights include steamed oysters wrapped in beef tataki (seared and thinly sliced beef) and basically anything barbecued on the robata. (☎02-6273 1424; www.lilotang.com.au; 1 Burbury Cl, Barton; mains $29-38; ⏰noon-2.30pm & 6-11pm Tue-Fri, 6-11pm Sat)

Chairman & Yip CHINESE $$$

12 ✖ MAP P48, F6

Chairman & Yip moved to this location on the corner of the Burbury Hotel in 2016, after 20 years in Civic. Locals may grumble at having to cross the lake to get their fix, but they still do it, because the classy, Cantonese-style

Her Majesty Queen Elizabeth II by John Dowie, Queen's Terrace Cafe

food is just that good. Go for the five-course tasting menu costing $88 per person with a two person minimum. (02-6162 1220; www. chairmangroup.com.au/chairmanyip; 1 Burbury Cl, Barton; mains $25-41; noon-12.30pm & 6-10.30pm Tue-Fri, 6-10.30pm Mon & Sat; P 🛜)

Bookplate   CAFE $$

In the foyer of the National Library (see 4 Map p48, E1) you'll find Bookplate, an award-winning cafe with a technicolour stained-glass backdrop. It's equally good as a lunch stop – with daily specials including pulled-pork tacos or poke bowls – or just for coffee and cake after a hard day hitting the books. The wine list is also excellent. (02-6262 1154; www.bookplate. com.au; National Library of Australia, Parkes Pl West, Parkes; dishes $16-25; 7.30am-5pm Mon-Thu, to 4pm Fri, from 9am Sat & Sun; 🍴)

Queen's Terrace Cafe   CAFE $$

13 🍴 MAP P48, D5

If Question Time has worn you down, stop for a bite at this (somewhat surprisingly) excellent cafe on the terrace above the main foyer. A wide range of fresh, well-prepared food is on offer, from rice-paper rolls to hearty bistro mains and everything in between. From Friday to Sunday high tea is available between noon and 4pm for $35 per person. (02-6277 5239; www.aph.gov.au; Parliament House, Parliament Dr, Capital Hill; dishes $10-26; 9am-4.30pm)

Outdoor Cinema

In summer, the Patrick White Lawns in front of the National Library (p51) host an open-air cinema, so you can enjoy the latest flicks while watching the sun set over Lake Burley Griffin. See www.openaircinemas. com.au for details.

Maple & Clove   CAFE $$

14 🍴 MAP P48, F6

Great coffee draws the crowds to this sleek cafe in the back blocks of Barton. Large sliding doors make the interior seem like an extension of the small grassy park next door. Come for fresh seasonal breakfasts and fabulous salads, like crisp apple with quinoa and broccolini. (02-6162 0777; www. mapleandclove.com.au; 7 Burbury Cl, Barton; dishes $14-25; 7.30am-3pm Mon-Fri, from 8am Sat & Sun; 🍴)

Ottoman   TURKISH $$$

15 🍴 MAP P48, G4

Set in an elegant garden pavilion, Ottoman has long been a favourite dining destination for Canberra's power brokers. Familiar dishes (meze, dolma, kofte) are given subtle contemporary twists, but for the most part they're left deliciously traditional. (02-6273 6111; www. ottomancuisine.com.au; 9 Broughton St, Barton; mains $31-36; noon-2.30pm & 6-10pm Tue-Fri, 6-10pm Sat)

Portrait Cafe

CAFE $

Rest your museum-weary feet at this petite cafe inside the National Portrait Gallery (see 1 ◉ Map p48, F2). A range of hot and cold dishes are on offer, as well as a tempting cake cabinet. (☎02-6102 7162; www. portrait.gov.au; National Portrait Gallery, King Edward Tce, Parkes; mains from $12.50; ⊙9am-4.30pm; ❄ 🛜)

Little Bird

CAFE $

16 ✕ MAP P48, G4

Sleek, bright Little Bird is a favoured caffeine dealer for public servants from nearby offices, who can be found slumped in front of its large windows all throughout the work week. Weekends are quieter, but the hearty breakfasts and friendly service are still as good. (www.littlebirdbarton.com; 48 Macquarie St, Barton; mains $8-22; ⊙7am-3pm Mon-Fri, 8am-2pm Sat & Sun)

Snappers

FISH & CHIPS $

17 ✕ MAP P48, A2

This tasty fish-and-chip shop on the bottom floor of a yacht club does a roaring trade on summer evenings. There is some seating available, but you may want to BYO picnic rug and find your own slice of lake view. (☎02-6273 1784; www.cscc.com. au/snapper; Mariner Pl, Yarralumla; fish & chips $14; ⊙11am-8pm Sep-May, to 3pm Mon-Fri, to 8pm Sat & Sun Jun-Aug)

Yogi's Kitchen

INDIAN $$

18 ✕ MAP P48, G4

A handy cheaper option in upmarket Barton, Yogi's Kitchen dishes

Street Café

up tasty, if mild, Indian dishes including all your usual faves such as butter chicken and dal makhani. Lunch specials ($12) are a particularly good deal. (📞0478 947 840; www.yogiskitchen.com.au; 5/48 Macquarie St, Barton; mains $16-19; ⏰11am-2.30pm & 5-9pm Mon-Sat)

Drinking

Ritual
COFFEE

19 ☕ MAP P48, E6

In the bottom of Little National Hotel (but entered through a separate door) this sleek cafe does a roaring trade with local public servants and office workers, who stampede down here every morning for their cup of coffee. Service is swift, the coffee is strong, and the sandwiches and baked goods are tasty and fresh. (📞0432 329 390; 21 National Circuit, Barton; ⏰7.30am-3.30pm Mon-Fri)

Ostani
BAR

20 ☕ MAP P48, F6

Tucked around the back of Hotel Realm, superchill Ostani has quickly become a favourite gathering spot for Barton residents. Drop by for an end-of-day drink on the jasmine-scented deck and you may end up lingering after sunset for wood-fired pizzas, gourmet burgers and other fancy pub grub. (📞02-6163 1802; www.ostani.com.au; 18 National Circuit, Barton; ⏰6.30am-late Mon-Fri, from 11am Sat & Sun)

High Tea at the Hyatt

If you're feeling decadent, indulge in scones and finger sandwiches at the **Hyatt Hotel** (Map p48, D2; 📞02-6270 1234; www.hyatt.com; 120 Commonwealth Ave, Yarralumla). Its renowned afternoon-tea buffet is held in the heritage-listed Tea Lounge from Friday to Sunday (per person $68).

Street Café
COFFEE

21 ☕ MAP P48, G3

Out the front of the National Gallery of Australia's (p40) main entrance, this little coffee stand pumps out excellent coffee as well as sandwiches and other portable snacks. Grab a flat white and head over to the sculpture garden. (www.nga.gov.au; National Gallery of Australia, Parkes Pl, Parkes; ⏰8am-2pm Mon-Fri, from 10am Sat & Sun, weather dependent)

Shopping

National Library Bookshop
BOOKS

Located in the National Library (see 4 ◎ Map p48, E1), this bookshop specialises in Australian books, but also has a good selection of recent titles and giftware. (📞02-6262 1424; http://bookshop.nla.gov.au; Parkes Pl, Parkes; ⏰10am-5pm)

Explore ✦

Acton

Home to the Australian National University and several government departments, leafy Acton bustles on weekdays but quietens down at night, when nearby Civic takes centre stage. The exception to this pattern is the relatively new minisuburb of New Acton, centred around the Nishi Building, which is home to more than its fair share of cafes, bars, restaurants and cinemas.

The Short List

○ **Australian National Botanic Gardens (p60)** *Strolling the lovely grounds, which include an actual rainforest (yes, in Canberra!).*

○ **National Museum of Australia (p64)** *Learning more about Australia's past and the history of the First Australians.*

○ **National Film & Sound Archive (p65)** *Perusing excellent temporary exhibitions at this small art-deco space.*

○ **Cupping Room (p66)** *Dining on seasonal breakfast options and supping fabulous coffee.*

○ **Black Market Bar (p68)** *Descending the dark elevator to stumble upon this excellent cocktail bar that feels like a well-kept secret.*

Getting There & Around

🏃 Acton and New Acton are only a short stroll from the main bus station and light rail stops in Civic.

🚌 Several buses service Acton, including route 53 to the National Museum.

🚗 Paid parking is available throughout Acton (from $3.10).

Neighbourhood Map on p62

National Museum of Australia (p64) DESIGNED BY ASHTON RAGGATT MCDOU-
GALL AND ROBERT PECK VON HARTEL TRETHOWAN/INAVANHATEREN/SHUTTERSTOCK ©

Top Sight 📷

Australian National Botanic Gardens

On the lower slopes of Black Mountain, these sprawling gardens showcase Australian floral diversity over 35 hectares of cultivated garden and 50 hectares of remnant bushland. Various themed routes are marked out, with the best introduction being the main path (45 minutes return), which takes in the eucalypt lawn, rock garden, rainforest gully and Sydney Region garden.

◉ MAP P62, B1

📞 02-6250 9588

www.nationalbotanic gardens.gov.au

Clunies Ross St

admission free

🕐 8.30am-5pm

Rainforest Gully

At the centre of the gardens, this lush, forested gully represents a horticultural triumph – tall trees provide a canopy for an entire rainforest ecosystem, despite Canberra's notoriously arid climate. The gully takes visitors on a tour of Australia's rainforests, starting with plants from Tasmania at the bottom and moving through species from Victoria and New South Wales as you ascend, ending with lush tropical plants from Queensland. The gully is also a haven for birdlife: be sure to keep an eye out for brightly coloured king parrots and crimson rosellas.

Rock Garden

Not just a garden of rocks, this carefully designed area uses raised rock beds to support a range of different soils, allowing plants from all over Australia to thrive in something resembling their natural environment. Look out for plants from alpine areas and desert-dwellers, as well as a lovely waterfall. Canberra's lizards also love this sunny spot, so you'll probably come across a few as you stroll through.

Red Centre Garden

Opened in 2013, this 4000-sq-metre area displays species from Australia's Red Centre. Over 800 tons of rock and 900 tons of red sand were transported here during construction of the garden, which incorporates sand dunes, rocky escarpments, shrublands and desert rivers. The garden is home to many iconic Australian plants, including ghost gums, Sturt's Desert Pea, mulga and spinifex grass. Look out for the large artwork *Grandmother's Country* (2013) by Indigenous Australian artist Teresa Pula McKeeman, which is the centrepiece of the garden's Central Meeting Place.

★ **Top Tips**

o Free hour-long guided walks depart from the visitor centre daily at 11am and 2pm.

o The gardens are host to all kinds of activities, talks, performances and events (especially during school holidays). Check online to see what's on during your stay.

o On very hot days, or during extreme weather conditions, some sections of the gardens may be closed.

✕ **Take a Break**

The elegant, airy **Pollen Cafe** (📞 02-6247 7321; www.pollen cafe.com.au; mains $16-25; ⏰ 9am-4pm, kitchen to 2.30pm) is nestled right in the heart of the gardens and is a great option for brekkie or lunch, with large, tasty meals and decent coffee.

If you prefer to bring your own lunch, the gardens offer plenty of lovely nooks and grassy knolls for picnics.

A

B

C

D

1

◀◉ 3

2◉

Australian National Botanic Gardens
◉

Daley Rd

Dickson Rd

Daley Rd

Clunies Ross St

Black Mountain Dr

Daley Rd

2

Black Mountain Nature Reserve

Sullivans Creek

ACTON

Australian National University

3

Parkes Way

Balmain Cres

Parkes Way

Lennox Crossing

4

Australian National University

Edinburgh Ave

Marcus Clarke St

Phillip Law St

10

9 ✕

14

6 ✕
21 🔒

16 ◉
Kendall La

20
🔒

5

11 ✕

12 ✕

NEW ACTON

19 ☆

0 ——————— 100 m

Parkes Way

6

Lake Burley Griffin

Lawson Cres

Ⓝ 0 ——————— 500 m
0 ——————— 0.25 miles

A

B

C

D

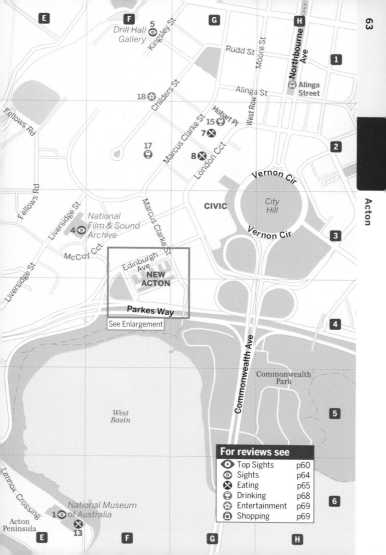

Acton

E
F
G
H

1
2
3
4
5
6

Drill Hall Gallery 5
Kingsley St
Rudd St
Moore St
Northbourne Ave
Alinga Street

Alinga St
West Row

Childers St
18
Hobart Pl
15
7
Marcus Clarke St
17
8
London Cct
Vernon Cir
CIVIC
City Hill
Vernon Cir

Fellows Rd

Liverside St
National Film & Sound Archive 4
Marcus Clarke St
McCoy Cct

Fellows Rd

Liverside St

Edinburgh Ave
NEW ACTON
Parkes Way
See Enlargement

Commonwealth Ave

Commonwealth Park

West Basin

Lennox Crossing

National Museum of Australia 1
13
Acton Peninsula

For reviews see

◉	Top Sights	p60
◉	Sights	p64
✕	Eating	p65
◉	Drinking	p68
✪	Entertainment	p69
🔒	Shopping	p69

Sights

National Museum of Australia

MUSEUM

1 MAP P62, E6

As well as telling Australia's national story, this museum hosts blockbuster touring exhibitions (admission prices vary). Highlights include the Gallery of First Australians, which explains the history and traditions of Aboriginal and Torres Strait Islander peoples, and the Garden of Australian Dreams, an interactive outdoor exhibition. The disjointed layout of the displays can sometimes be confusing; take a one-hour guided tour (adult/child $15/10, 10am, 1pm and 3pm daily) to get the best out of the museum. (☎02-6208 5000; www.nma.gov.au; Lawson Cres, Acton Peninsula; admission free; ☺9am-5pm)

Black Mountain

NATURE RESERVE

2 MAP P62, B1

On the western side of the city, the forested slopes of Black Mountain (812m) provide some easily accessible bushland perfect for bushwalking and mountain biking. The most common hike is the two-hour (2km) Summit Walk, which ends at the Telstra Tower, however there are several other well-marked trails to explore. Pick up a brochure at the visitor centre (p142) before you set out. (www.environment.act.gov.au/parks-conservation/parks-and-reserves; Mitchell)

Black Mountain

Telstra Tower

VIEWPOINT

3 MAP P62, A1

Black Mountain, northwest of the city, is topped by the oddly stumpy 195m-high Telstra Tower, which offers a sweeping vista from its 66m-high viewing gallery.

The tower is visible across most of the city and makes a useful navigational landmark. (Black Mountain Tower; ☑02-6219 6120; www.telstratower.com.au; 100 Black Mountain Dr; adult/child $7.50/3; ☉9am-10pm)

National Film & Sound Archive

LIBRARY

4 MAP P62, E3

Set in a delightful art-deco building (look for the stained-glass platy-pus in the foyer dome), this archive preserves Australian moving-picture and sound recordings. The gallery space stages free tempo-rary exhibitions on Australian film history. There's also a cute little theatre where documentaries are played and the larger Arc Cinema, used for special screenings and film festivals; check the website for show times.

The courtyard is also home to a very pleasant cafe. (☑02-6248 2000; www.nfsa.gov.au; McCoy Circuit; admission free; ☉9am-5pm Mon-Thu, to 8pm Fri, noon-5pm Sat & Sun)

Drill Hall Gallery

GALLERY

5 MAP P62, F1

The Australian National University's main gallery displays

Summer Concerts

On weekends in January and February the eucalypt lawn in the **botanic gardens** (p60) plays host to the Summer Sounds concert series, with live music echoing across the gardens as the sun sets.

special exhibitions and items from the ANU's art collection. On permanent display is the collection's highlight: the nine large luminous painted panels that comprise *Riverbend*, where Sidney Nolan's famous stylised Ned Kelly is hidden within the muted pinks, greens and browns of the Australian bush. (☑02-6125 5832; http://dhg.anu.edu.au; Kingsley St; admission free; ☉10am-5pm Wed-Sun Mar-Nov)

Eating

Fekerte's Ethiopian

ETHIOPIAN $

6 MAP P62, A5

Operating out of a hole in the wall of the Nishi Building, Fekerte's serves authentic Ethiopian cuisine to clamouring office workers and ANU students at lunch. Several meat and vegetarian dishes are available each day, served either with rice or injera bread. (Nishi Bldg, 25 Edinburgh Ave, New Acton; dishes $10-12; ☉11.30am-3pm Mon-Fri; 🥗)

Two Before Ten
CAFE $

7 ⊗ MAP P62, G2

Breaking from the Australian tradition that says good cafes should be bohemian and battered looking, this airy place brings a touch of Cape Cod to the centre of a city block. The excellent coffee comes from its own roastery in Aranda, where there is also another outpost of the cafe. (www.twobeforeten.com.au; 1 Hobart Pl, Acton; mains $11-18; ⊙7am-4pm Mon-Fri, 8am-2pm Sat & Sun)

Cupping Room
CAFE $$

8 ⊗ MAP P62, G2

Queues often form outside this airy corner cafe, drawn by the prospect of Canberra's best coffee and an interesting menu, including great vegetarian and vegan options. The seasonal chia pudding is extraordinary, but if you prefer something a little more familiar, the burgers are equally as delicious. Choose your coffee blend from the tasting notes; we recommend the filter coffee. (☎02-6257 6412; www.thecuppingroom.com.au; 1 University Ave, Civic; mains $11-25; ⊙7am-4pm Mon-Fri, 8am-3pm Sat & Sun; ⊿)

Morning Glory
CAFE $$

9 ⊗ MAP P62, B5

Nestled in the heart of the New Acton complex, this sprawling cafe has a sleek, contemporary vibe and is a popular coffee stop for local office workers. The menu offers modern cafe dishes with an Asian twist, like black sesame and milk-tea pancake waffles at breakfast, or soba salad with wakame seaweed and enoki mushrooms at lunch. (☎02-6257 6464; www.morning-glory.com.au; 2/15 Edinburgh Ave, New Acton; dishes $12-27; ⊙6am-3pm; ❄🛜)

Bicicletta
ITALIAN $$

10 ⊗ MAP P62, B4

This friendly Italian restaurant is part of the Peppers hotel complex, but it doesn't feel like a generic hotel bistro. Tables spill out into a colourful courtyard where shady trees and potted plants provide a subtly Mediterranean vibe, and the food is much the same – traditional Italian with a Canberra twist. (☎02-6175 2222; www.bicicletta.com.au; 1/15 Edinburgh Ave, New Acton; mains breakfast $12-23, lunch $18-25, dinner $21-36; ⊙6.30-10.30am, noon-3pm & 5-10pm Mon-Fri, from 7am Sat & Sun)

Monster Kitchen & Bar
MODERN AUSTRALIAN $$

11 ⊗ MAP P62, A5

Concealed in the ubercool Nishi Building, Monster is one of Canberra's more versatile dining spots. Hotel guests, New Acton locals and politicians alike check their Instagram feeds over breakfast. Shared plates with a subtle Middle Eastern influence get everyone talking during lunch and dinner. At night it morphs into a bar (and is a good place to overhear political gossip).

There's good seating by the large fires but a separate dining room overlooks the lake for some of the city's best views. (📞02-6287 6287; www.monsterkitchen.com.au; Hotel Hotel, 25 Edinburgh Ave, New Acton; breakfast $11-20, shared plates $20-34; 🕑6.30am-late; P 📶)

Močan & Green Grout

 CAFE $$

12 🍴 MAP P62, B5

Often awash with morning sunshine, this sophisticated New Acton cafe with an open kitchen is one of Canberra's best places to start the day. Free-range-this and local-that feature on the concise

Ngunnawal Country

Canberra is built on Ngunnawal country. The Ngunnawal people are the Indigenous Australian nation that lived on the land around Canberra at the time of European settlement, along with the Gundungurra to the north, the Ngarigo to the south, the Yuin to the west, and the Wiradjuri to the east. Rock paintings found in nearby Tharwa indicate that Indigenous Australians have lived in this region for at least 20,000 years, though evidence from nearby regions suggests an even longer duration.

The Ngunnawal people called this place Kanberra, believed to mean 'Meeting Place'. The name was probably derived from huge intertribal gatherings that happened annually when large numbers of bogong moths – a popular food source – appeared in the region.

The Ngunnawal way of life was violently disrupted following the arrival of Europeans in 1820, when settlers began to move into the Canberra basin, bringing sheep and other introduced species. Indigenous Australians resisted the intrusion of the graziers, most notably in 1826 when over a thousand people gathered at Lake George to protest their displacement. Despite their efforts, the Aboriginal inhabitants of the area were gradually forced further north as their hunting grounds were diminished by the actions of the settlers, and by the 1860s very few remained in the area.

During the first stage of European settlement, the Canberra area was part of the colony of New South Wales. In 1901, when Australia's separate colonies federated, the rivalry between Sydney and Melbourne meant neither could become the new nation's capital, so a location between the two cities was carved out of southern NSW as a compromise. This new city was officially named Canberra in 1913, and became the national capital in 1927.

seasonal menu. (☎02-6162 2909; www.mocanandgreengrout.com; 19 Marcus Clarke St, New Acton; mains breakfast & lunch $10-18, shared plates dinner $18-30; ⊙7am-6pm Mon, to 9pm Tue-Sat, 8am-4pm Sun; 📶🍴)

National Museum of Australia Cafe
CAFE $$

13  MAP P62, E6

Set in a glass-roofed atrium overlooking the lake, this cafeteria-style cafe is a great spot to combat museum fatigue. Meals are a cut above normal cafeteria food – think fresh salads and barra burgers. (☎02-6208 5179; www.nma.gov.au; National Museum of Australia, Lawson Cres, Acton Peninsula; ⊙8.30am-4.45pm; P❄📶)

Drinking

Black Market Bar
COCKTAIL BAR

14 🚇 MAP P62, B5

Behind a hidden doorway, descend in the lift to the basement to find Black Market, a dimly lit and atmospheric basement bar with killer cocktails and a speakeasy vibe. It's the perfect spot for a late-evening digestif. (www.blackmarket. bar; 2 Phillip Law St, New Acton; ⊙4pm-midnight Tue-Wed, to 1am Thu, to 2am Fri & Sat)

88mph
BAR

15 🚇 MAP P62, G2

Party like it's 1985 at 88mph (named for the speed the DeLorean had to reach to time travel in *Back to the Future*). A

National Museum of Australia Cafe

neon pulsing dance floor, cocktails on tap and a supremely kitsch playlist all combine to wake you up before you go-go. Wear your dancing shoes.

If you want to do more than just dance, there are three karaoke rooms out the back with a healthy serve of cheesy pop on the menu. (www.88mph.bar; 8-10 Hobart Pl, Civic; ⊙6pm-2am Tue-Wed, 4pm-4am Thu-Sat)

Parlour Wine Room
WINE BAR

16 ⊜ MAP P62, B5

Modern banquettes share the polished wooden floor with well-stuffed chesterfield lounges at this contemporary take on a Victorian smoking lounge. Stop in for an Aperol spritz on the deck overlooking the lake or pop inside for champagne and oysters. (☑02-6257 7325; www.parlour.net.au; 16 Kendall Lane, New Acton; ⊙noon-late)

Wig & Pen
MICROBREWERY

17 ⊜ MAP P62, F2

Tucked away at the side of the Australian National University's School of Music, this long-standing Canberra brewpub is a little atmosphere-deficient inside but spills out onto a leafy terrace. (☑02-6248 0171; www.facebook.com/wigandpen.canberra; 100 Childers St, Llewellyn Hall, Civic; ⊙11.30am-9pm Mon-Thu, to midnight Fri, from 2pm Sat, to 7pm Sun)

Entertainment

Street Theatre
THEATRE

18 ⭐ MAP P62, F1

Canberra's leading independent theatre stages interesting contemporary performances from new and established practitioners. (☑02-6247 1223; www.thestreet.org.au; 15 Childers St, Civic; ⊙box office 10am-3pm Mon-Fri)

Palace Electric
CINEMA

19 ⭐ MAP P62, A5

A luxe cinema in the Nishi Building that screens mainly art-house and independent films. (☑02-6222 4900; www.palacecinemas.com.au; 2 Phillip Law St, New Acton; adult/child $19/13.50; ⊙10am-10pm)

Shopping

Curatoreum
GIFTS & SOUVENIRS

20 🔒 MAP P62, B5

A lovely gift- and bookshop that's just as well curated as its name would suggest. It's a great place to pick up a unique gift. (www.thecuratoreum.com; 12 Kendall Lane, New Acton; ⊙9.30am-5.30pm Mon-Thu, to 6.30pm Fri & Sat, 10am-3pm Sun)

Cellar Door Market
MARKET

21 🔒 MAP P62, A5

Every week different local wineries pop up at this market held in the foyer of the Nishi Building, offering tastings and selling wine at cellar-door prices. (Nishi Bldg, 25 Edinburgh Ave, New Acton; ⊙3-6pm Sat).

Top Sight 📷

National Arboretum

Canberra's National Arboretum is an ever-developing showcase of trees from around the world, with 94 forests of different species on display. It is early days for many of the plantings, but it's still worth visiting for the spectacular visitor centre and excellent views over the city. Regular guided tours are informative, and there is a brilliant adventure playground for kids.

📞 02-6207 8484

www.nationalarboretum.act.gov.au

Forest Dr, Weston Creek

admission free

🕐 6am-8.30pm Oct-Mar, 7am-5.30pm Apr-Sep, village centre 9am-4pm

Village Centre

Find out all about the various plantings and pick up maps and other information at the Village Centre at the heart of the arboretum. The centre encompasses multimedia displays, two cafes, a gift shop and the Pod Playground – a fabulous adventure playground with all kinds of interestingly designed equipment, including a series of cubbies designed to look like acorns.

National Bonsai & Penjing Collection

To the side of the Village Centre you'll find the National Bonsai Collection, a fascinating display featuring dozens of bonsai and *penjing* trees (*penjing* is the Chinese word for the cultivation of miniature trees). Aluminium or copper wire is used to shape the growth of the trees, some of which are over 60 years old. As well as the traditional cypress and pine, the collection features plants you may not have seen grown this way before, including flowering azaleas and a magnificent river red gum.

Wide Brown Land

The most Instagrammed spot in the arboretum is the *Wide Brown Land* (2010) sculpture, based on the line from Dorothea Mackellar's famous poem 'My Country'. The sculpture springs from Mackellar's handwriting and was made from steel by Marcus Tatton, Futago Design Studios and Chris Viney. You'll find it near the Himalayan cedar forest as you drive into the park.

Lookout

At the top of Dairy Farmers Hill (turn left up Forest Dr as you enter the arboretum) this lookout offers spectacular views over Canberra and beyond. A one-hour (2km) walking circuit departs from the Village Centre to take in the lookout and surrounding forest.

★ **Top Tips**

◦ Free 20-minute guided talks depart from the desk in the Village Centre daily on the hour between 10am and 3pm.

◦ On Wednesdays at 11am, Saturdays at 2pm and Sundays at 11am, hour-long guided forest walks take you deeper into the site.

✕ **Take a Break**

Inside the Village Centre, the friendly **Sprout Cafe** (dishes $7-15; ⏱9am-4pm) offers fresh, simple food and drinks.

Nearby, the **Conservatory** (☎02-6130 0173; ⏱noon-2pm Mon-Fri, from 8am Sat & Sun) offers set two- or three-course lunches ($42/52), and a la carte breakfasts on weekends.

★ **Getting There**

🚌 Catch bus 180 or 181 from the Civic bus interchange.

🚗 The Arboretum is 8km (around a 15-minute drive) from the city centre.

Explore ⬡

Civic

The geographical and figurative centre of Canberra's business district, Civic abounds with shops, cafes, restaurants and bars. During the day most places cater to a business crowd, while after dark this area is the heart of Canberra's nightlife scene. You'll find plenty of things to do and see, with several smaller sights in the vicinity as well as the must-visit Australian War Memorial. There are also some lovely sections of lakeshore perfectly designed for strolling.

The Short List

○ **Australian War Memorial (p74)** *Paying homage to the many Australian lives lost in conflict at this sobering memorial and museum.*

○ **Lake Burley Griffin (p78)** *Strolling, running, cycling or skating the peaceful, paved shore of this stunning artificial lake.*

○ **National Capital Exhibition (p79)** *Learning about how Canberra came to be Australia's capital at this well-designed museum inside the visitor centre.*

○ **Bar Rochford (p84)** *Sipping local wines at one of Canberra's best bars amid a cosmopolitan atmosphere.*

○ **No Name Lane (p83)** *Tasting the city's best doughnuts as well as a plethora of other delicious treats at this foodie hotspot.*

Getting There & Around

🚋 Alinga St.

🚌 Many bus lines start and end in Civic.

🚗 There are numerous parking lots scattered around, including a handy one at the Canberra Centre.

Neighbourhood Map on p76

Lake Burley Griffin at sunrise (p78) DAVID TAO/SHUTTERSTOCK ©

Top Sight 📷
Australian War Memorial

Canberra's glorious art-deco war memorial is a highlight in a city filled with interesting architecture. Built to commemorate WWI, 'the war to end all wars', it opened its doors in 1941 when the next world war was already well underway. Attached to the memorial is a large, exceptionally well-designed museum devoted to the nation's military history.

◎ MAP P76, G3
📞 02-6243 4211
www.awm.gov.au
Treloar Cres, Campbell
admission free
🕙 10am-5pm

Hall of Memory

At the heart of the War Memorial, the Hall of Memory is a Byzantine-inspired domed chapel with soaring stained-glass windows. At its centre lies the Tomb of the Unknown Soldier. The soldier interred in the tomb died in France during WWI and was repatriated and reburied here in 1993. The tomb is intended to commemorate all those who did not return home from war and whose final resting places are still unknown.

Roll of Honour

All along the corridors leading to the Hall of Memory, huge brass plaques record the names of more than 102,000 members of the Australian armed services who have died during wartime. Viewing the line upon line of names is a sobering experience. Visitors who wish to locate the names of particular people can search the Roll of Honour database, available on the memorial's website, which shows the location of every name on the roll.

Dioramas

Nine large dioramas are scattered throughout the WWI exhibits. They were first conceived in the 1920s as a way of showing visitors to the memorial the true horror and devastation of the battlefields. Among them are images of battles whose names have become common parlance – including Lone Pine, the Somme and Pozières. The dioramas remain an eerie, moving insight into the utter bleakness of war.

Anzac Hall

At the far end of the memorial, this enormous hangar displays five aircraft and a submarine. The stories of each of the displays are told through arresting sound and light shows that begin on the hour, every hour. One such display, *Sydney Under Attack,* tells the story of the three midget submarines that raided Sydney Harbour in 1942, sinking the depot-ship *HMAS Kuttabul.*

★ **Top Tips**

○ Free guided tours depart at least hourly between 10am and 3pm, with various options from one to 1½ hours available.

○ The child-friendly Discovery Zone is only open to the public on weekdays between 12.30pm and 1.30pm, but is open all day on weekends and during the school holidays. (During the week, it is reserved for visiting school groups.)

✖ **Take a Break**

In a grand concrete pavilion off to the side of the memorial, **Poppy's Cafe** (☎02-6262 7380; www.awm.gov.au/visit/poppys; mains $10-21; ⏱8.30am-4.30pm) serves basic cafe-style food like sandwiches, hot chips and cakes.

On the mezzanine of Anzac Hall, the smaller **Landing Place Cafe** (www.awm.gov.au; dishes $8-17; ⏱10.30am-4.30pm) also offers meals and refreshments to museum-weary visitors.

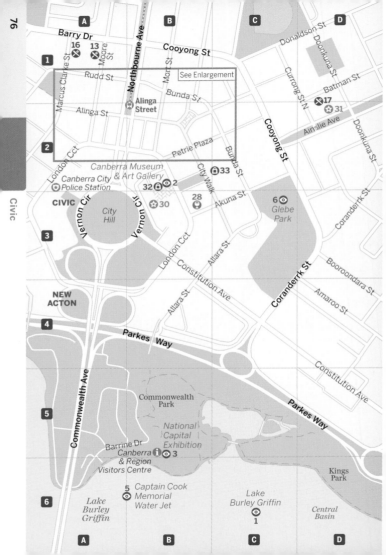

Barry Dr
16
13
Moore St
Northbourne Ave
Cooyong St
Donaldson St
Doonkuna St
D
A
B
C
1
Marcus Clarke St
Rudd St
Mort St
Bunda St
Currong St N
Batman St
17
31
Alinga Street
Alinga St
Ainslie Ave
Doonkuna St
London Cct
Petrie Plaza
2
Bunda St
Cooyong St
33
City Walk
Canberra Museum
& Art Gallery
32
2
Canberra City
Police Station
28
Akuna St
6
Glebe
Park
CIVIC
30
Vernon Cir
City
Hill
Vernon Cir
Coranderrk St
3
London Cct
Allara St
Constitution Ave
Booroondara St
NEW
ACTON
Allara St
Constitution Ave
Coranderrk St
Amaroo St
4
Parkes Way
Constitution Ave
5
Parkes Way
Commonwealth
Park
Commonwealth Ave
National
Capital
Exhibition
Kings
Park
Barrine Dr
Canberra
& Region
Visitors Centre
3
6
Lake
Burley
Griffin
5
Captain Cook
Memorial
Water Jet
Lake
Burley Griffin
1
Central
Basin
A
B
C
D

Civic

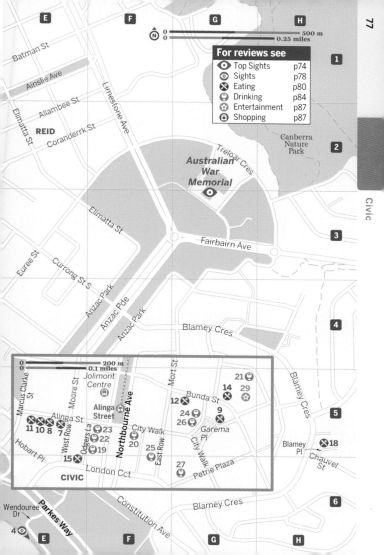

Batman St

Ainslie Ave

Allambee St

Elmatta St

Elmatta St

REID

Coranderrk St

Limestone Ave

Euree St

Treloar Cres

Canberra Nature Park

Australian War Memorial

Elimatta St

Currong St S

Anzac Park

Anzac Pde

Anzac Park

Fairbairn Ave

Blamey Cres

Blamey Cres

Blamey Cres

Jolimont Centre

Marcus Clarke St

Moore St

Alinga St

Alinga Street

Northbourne Ave

Mort St

Bunda St

City Walk

East Row

City Walk

Garema Pl

Blamey Pl

Chauvel St

11 10 8

West Row

Odgers La

7

9

12

24

26

21

14

29

18

23

22

19

20

25

27

15

Hobart Pl

London Cct

CIVIC

Constitution Ave

Blamey Cres

Wendouree Dr

Parkes Way

4

Sights

Lake Burley Griffin LAKE

1 ◉ MAP P76, C6

This ornamental lake was created in 1963 when the 33m-high Scrivener Dam was erected on the Molonglo River. It's lined with important institutions and monuments, including the National Carillon and Captain Cook Memorial Water Jet (p80).

You can cycle the entire 28km perimeter in two hours or walk it in seven. Alternatively, you can make a smaller 'loop' by making use of the two bridges – the popular central loop is 5km and can be walked in one to 1½ hours. See the detailed walk, p88.

Canberra Museum & Art Gallery MUSEUM

2 ◉ MAP P76, B2

This local museum is worth visiting for the Sidney Nolan paintings alone – 141 works, including canvases from his *Ned Kelly* series and *Burke and Wills Expedition* were gifted to the Australian government in 1974, and a rotating collection is on display here. There's also an exhibition on Canberra's own story, which is often overshadowed by 'national' stories, as well as a variety of interesting and unusual temporary exhibitions – when we last visited, there was one solely devoted to snow globes.

The gallery staff give good floor talks, and there are also fun activities for kids – check the website

Lake Burley Griffin

Creating Lake Burley Griffin

Though it might seem at first glance that Canberra was built around the sparkling waters of Lake Burley Griffin, the reality is actually the other way around. The concept of an artificial lake was part of the original design of the nation's capital as early as 1909, however it wasn't until 1961, with the excavation of the lake floor and the damming of the Molonglo River at Scrivener Dam, that Lake Burley Griffin finally came into existence. Even then, the final stages of construction were hampered by a prolonged period of drought, which meant that the lake did not reach its planned water level until 1964, when it was officially inaugurated by then Prime Minister Sir Robert Menzies. A statue of Menzies, who championed the lake project throughout his prime ministership, can be seen when strolling along the lake shore near Nerang Pool.

to see what's on during your visit. The museum cafe is also very pleasant. (CMAG; ☎02-6207 3968; www.cmag.com.au; cnr London Circuit & Civic Sq, Civic; admission free; ⏱10am-5pm Mon-Sat)

National Capital Exhibition

MUSEUM

3 ◉ MAP P76, B5

This small but fascinating museum tells the story of how Canberra came to be Australia's capital. Displays include reproductions of the drawings entered in the international competition to design the city, including the exquisite watercolour renderings of the winning design created by Marion Mahony Griffin, the often overlooked wife and creative partner of Walter Burley Griffin. The glass pavilion offers lovely views over the lake and Capital Hill, so you can see the real-life outcomes of the plans you're perusing. (☎02-6272 2902; www.nationalcapital.gov.au; Barrine Dr, Commonwealth Park; admission free; ⏱9am-5pm)

National Carillon

TOWER

4 ◉ MAP P76, E6

This 50m-high bell tower was opened in 1970 as a gift from Britain on Canberra's 50th anniversary. The tower has 55 bronze bells, weighing from 7kg to 6 tonnes each, making it one of the world's largest musical instruments. The bells mark the hour and there's usually a recital at 12.30pm on Wednesday and Sunday.

The carillon is scheduled to undergo restoration work throughout 2019 ahead of its 50th anniversary in 2020, when a year-long celebratory program of performances will be held. (www.nca.gov.au; Aspen Island, Lake Burley Griffin)

Glebe Park Events

Tucked around the back of the Canberra Centre, away from most of Civic's bustle, the spacious lawns and leafy elm trees of Glebe Park make it the perfect location for many of Canberra's favourite local events. In the weeks leading up to Christmas the park is home to decorations, stalls and live music, while at other times it plays host to everything from Diwali celebrations to Reconciliation Day performances. Visit www.events.act.gov.au to see what's on.

Captain Cook Memorial Water Jet
LANDMARK

5 MAP P76, B6

Built in 1970 to mark the bicentenary of British explorer James Cook's landfall, this memorial near Regatta Point consists of a 6-tonne column of water shooting up to 152m into the air. After many years of troubles, the jet was extensively refurbished in 2017 (at a cost of $3 million) and now operates daily between 11am and 2pm. There is also a skeleton globe on the shore on which Cook's three great voyages are traced. (Captain Cook's Fountain; Lake Burley Griffin)

Glebe Park
PARK

6 MAP P76, C3

This spacious green park is filled with leafy elm trees that turn a lovely golden yellow in autumn. There's a playground for kids and lots of paved paths for wandering – a perfect antidote to nearby Canberra Centre's (p87) bustle. (Coranderrk St, Civic; 7am-8pm Apr-Sep, to 10pm Oct-Mar)

Eating

Baby Su
ASIAN $

7 MAP P76, E5

Neon lights and diner booths give Baby Su a more casual feel than its big sister Lazy Su (p94) in Braddon, but the same attention to detail presides. Drop in for delicious Asian-inspired burgers, fried chicken and distinctive 'waffle-cut' fries. The Lucky Pack ($20) with a burger, fries, chicken and a soft drink, is particularly good value. (www.baby-su.com.au; cnr No Name Lane, West Row & Alinga St; burgers $12, other mains $15-21; noon-10pm)

Taco Taco
TACOS $

8 MAP P76, E5

Fabulous Mexican-inspired food is the name of the game at this bright, friendly corner spot in the No Name Lane precinct. The menu changes regularly but always offers fresh, seasonal tacos and other bean-and-chilli-style dishes. There's also house-made sodas and horchata (a spiced, milk-based drink) as well as a compact wine, beer and cocktail list. (www.tacotacocbr.com; Shop 8, 40 Marcus Clarke St, No Name Lane; tacos from $7, other dishes $12-15; ⊙noon-3pm Mon, noon-3pm & 5pm-late Tue-Fri, 5pm-late Sat)

Selli's
SANDWICHES $

9 ⊗ MAP P76, G5

Black-and-white tiles and neon lights give this American-style diner an air of authenticity, an impression supported by the topping-laden burgers, sandwiches, hot dogs and other mouth-watering dishes that fly out the door at lunch. At breakfast the menu switches to bagels – we like the 'Sunshine', with lemon ricotta, peach slices, blueberries and honey. (☎02-5105 3114; www.sellicatessen.com.au; Shop 5, 88 Bunda St; mains $11-15; ⊙8am-3pm Mon-Thu, to late Sat, 10am-5pm Sun)

Doughnut Dept
BAKERY $

10 ⊗ MAP P76, E5

Polished concrete and brass accents give this bright cafe a classy, industrial vibe, but we'd come here even if the floor was made of mud – the doughnuts are that good. from rhubarb and pomegranate to tiramisu and cinnamon sugar. There's also a small menu (think granola, toasties), but we all know what we're really here for. (www.thedoughnutdept.com.au; No Name Lane, 2 Alinga St; doughnuts $5; ⊙7.30am-5pm Mon-Thu, to late Fri)

Captain Cook Memorial Water Jet

Terra
AUSTRALIAN $$

11 🍴 MAP P76, E5

By day this atmospheric, contemporary space churns out delectable seasonal brunch dishes and fabulous coffee. At night the rotisserie takes centre stage, with six-hour roasted meats alongside innovative sides like fried cauliflower or baked potatoes with miso. The best option, though, is the 'Feed Me' set menu (minimum two people) – trust us, you won't go home hungry. (📞02-6230 4414; www.terracanberra.com.au; Shop G2, No Name Lane, 40 Marcus Clarke St; mains breakfast & lunch $10-16, dinner $18-30, set menu per person $58; ⏱7.30am-4pm Mon-Wed, to late Thu & Fri, 10.30am-late Sat)

Akiba
ASIAN $$

12 🍴 MAP P76, G5

A high-octane vibe pervades this superslick pan-Asian place, fuelled by a lively young crew that effortlessly splashes together cocktails, dispenses food recommendations and juggles orders without breaking a sweat. A raw bar serves delectable sashimi, freshly shucked oysters and zingy ceviche. Salt-and-Sichuan-pepper squid and pork-belly buns are crowd pleasers, and we love the Japanese-style eggplant. (📞02-6162 0602; www.akiba.com.au; 40 Bunda St; noodle & rice dishes $10-21, share plates $16-33; ⏱11.30am-midnight Sun-Wed, to 2am Thu-Sat)

Courgette

Temporada

MODERN AUSTRALIAN **$$**

13 MAP P76, A1

The bar is front and centre at this industrial-looking multipurpose place, which transitions from cafe to bistro to restaurant to bar as the day progresses. (📞02-6249 6683; www.temporada.com.au; 15 Moore St; mains breakfast $8-18, lunch $18-38, dinner $22-45; ⏰7.30am-late Mon-Fri, from 5pm Sat)

Sammy's Kitchen

MALAYSIAN **$$**

14 MAP P76, G5

This long-standing local favourite became a little more upmarket when it crossed the street into new premises, but the generously proportioned Chinese and Malay dishes are unchanged. (📞02-6247 1464; www.sammyskitchen.com.au; 9 Bunda St; mains $16-25; ⏰11.30am-2.30pm & 5-10.30pm Mon-Thu, to 11.30pm Fri & Sat, to 10pm Sun; 🖊)

Lemon Grass

THAI **$$**

15 MAP P76, E6

This dependable Thai institution offers a long list of vegetarian, stir-fry, curry and seafood dishes. You can bring your own wine (corkage $3), and if you're a fan of king prawns order the *goong gratiam* (garlic prawns) with pepper and steamed vegetables. (📞02-6247 2779; www.lemongrassthai.com.au; 65 London Circuit; mains $17-19; ⏰noon-2.30pm & 5-10.30pm Mon-Fri, 5-10.30pm Sat; 🖊)

No Name Lane

Civic's newest dining hotspot is the small block on its western edge bordered by Alinga and Marcus Clarke Sts. Centred around the elusive-sounding No Name Lane, this tiny strip packs a gastronomic punch at both lunch and dinner, with highlights including Baby Su (p80), Terra, Taco Taco (p80) and Doughnut Dept (p81).

Courgette

MODERN AUSTRALIAN **$$$**

16 MAP P76, A1

With its crisp white linen, impeccable service and discreet but expensive ambience, Courgette is the kind of place to bring someone you want to impress, like a date, or perhaps the Finnish ambassador. The exacting standards continue with the precisely prepared, exquisitely plated and flavour-laden food. (📞02-6247 4042; www.courgette.com.au; 54 Marcus Clarke St; 3-course lunch $66, 4-course dinner $88; ⏰noon-3pm & 6-11pm Mon-Sat)

Sage

MODERN AUSTRALIAN **$$$**

17 MAP P76, D1

In the genteel environs of the Gorman House Arts Centre, Sage offers well-regarded degustation-style dining; the five-course chef's tasting menu is worth the splurge. Service is discreet and never rushed. In summer the courtyard blossoms with **Mint**, a cocktail bar that makes for a perfect outdoor drink. (📞02-6249 6050; www.sagerestaurant.net.au; Batman St, Braddon; 3-course lunch/dinner $65/79, 5-course tasting menu $95; ⏰noon-2pm & 6-11pm Tue-Sat; 🚲)

Lanterne Rooms
MALAYSIAN $$$

18 🍴 MAP P76, H5

Serving expertly cooked Nyonya dishes in a colourful dining room referencing Penang farmhouses from the colonial era, Lanterne Rooms is sophisticated and welcoming. Visit during the day to take advantage of the excellent-value market lunch for $19. (📞02-6249 6889; www.chairmangroup.com.au; Blamey Pl, Campbell; mains lunch $27-34, dinner $29-38; ⏰noon-2.30pm & 6-10pm Tue-Fri, 6-10pm Sat)

Drinking

Molly
BAR

19 🚇 MAP P76, F5

The doorway to this little gem, hidden away down quiet Odgers Lane, is illuminated only by a light bulb. It may take some courage to push through the unmarked wooden door, but have faith; inside you'll find an atmospheric 1920s-style speakeasy, with dim lighting, cosy booths and a very impressive whisky selection. Try the cocktails. (www.molly.bar; Odgers Lane; ⏰4pm-midnight Mon-Wed, to 2am Thu-Sat, 5pm-late Sun)

Bar Rochford
WINE BAR

Bearded barmen concentrate earnestly on their cocktail

Canberra Theatre Centre (p87)

LINCOLN FOWLER/ALAMY STOCK ©

Hidden Bars

Civic has the highest concentration of bars and nightlife in Canberra, so you'll find something to suit every taste, from sophisticated wine bars to friendly pubs and everything in between. Finding Canberra's best drinking dens can be a bit of a treasure hunt, and never more so than down seemingly quiet Odgers Lane. If you enter the nondescript doorway with naught but a light above it you'll find Molly, an atmospheric 1920s-style speakeasy, while climbing the fire escape at the Alinga St end will bring you to Highball Express, a rollicking Cuban-themed cocktail bar.

constructions and wine recommendations at this sophisticated but unstuffy bar in the Melbourne Building, also housing Thai restaurant Lemon Grass (see **15** Map p76, E6). Dress up and hope for a table by one of the big arched windows.

In 2017, *Australian Gourmet Traveller* named Rochford its 'bar of the year' putting it onto the itineraries of most visitors to Canberra. (☏02-6230 6222; www.barrochford.com; 1st fl, 65 London Circuit; ☺5pm-late Tue-Thu, 3pm-1am Fri, from 5pm Sat)

Brew Nation
CRAFT BEER

20 MAP P76, F5

The interior might look a bit stark (some might say modern) but this friendly bar has nine local beers on tap and many more in cans and bottles besides, making it the perfect spot to try a local brew. (www.brewnation.com.au; 103 Alinga St; ☺4pm-midnight Tue-Sat)

Coffee Lab
COFFEE

21 MAP P76, G5

Tired shoppers seeking a caffeine fix near the Canberra Centre (p87) should look no further than Coffee Lab, where smooth brews are dispensed to clamouring crowds all day long. There are also tasty breakfasts and a tempting cake cabinet. (www.thecoffeelab.com.au; 26 Narellan Pl, Canberra Centre; breakfast $13-17; ☺7am-4pm)

Highball Express
COCKTAIL BAR

22 MAP P76, F5

There's no sign, so take a punt and climb the fire escape in the lane behind Smith's Alternative to this louche tropical take on a 1920s Cuban rum bar. The highball cocktails are excellent and often come served with banana chips. (www.highballexpress.com.au; Level 1, 82 Alinga St; ☺4pm-late Tue-Sat)

Smith's Alternative
BAR

23 🕒 MAP P76, F5

When the legendary Smith's Alternative Bookshop closed down, it turned out that the name worked just as well for its successor. The new Smith's is an arty cafe-bar and performance space, with a makeshift stage in one corner and cakes in the cabinet. In the evenings, expect to be bemused by anything from live music to slam poetry to theatre. (📞02-6257 1225; www.smithsalternative.com; 76 Alinga St; 🕒8am-midnight Mon-Thu, to late Fri, 9am-late Sat, noon-midnight Sun)

Hippo Co
BAR

24 🕒 MAP P76, G5

This cosy upstairs lounge-bar is popular with young whisky and cocktail slurpers who file in for Wednesday-night jazz – the turntable rules other evenings. The gin and whisky lists are more than impressive; ask the friendly bartenders for their recommendation. (📞02-6247 7555; www.hippoco.com. au; Level 1, 17 Garema Pl; 🕒5pm-late Mon-Thu & Sat, from 4pm Fri)

Charming Chimes

While you're strolling around Lake Burley Griffin, stop by the National Carillon (p79) at 12.30pm on Wednesdays or Sundays for a free bell-ringing recital.

Phoenix
PUB

25 🕒 MAP P76, F6

The studenty Phoenix is a staunch supporter of local music, with bands playing around four nights a week. On other nights you might strike a comedian, a poet or a pub quiz. The atmosphere is friendly and collegiate. (📞02-6169 5092; www.lovethephoenix.com; 23 East Row; 🕒5pm-1am Mon-Wed, to 3am Thu-Sat)

Honky Tonks
BAR

26 🕒 MAP P76, G5

Canberra's compadres meet here to eat tacos, drink margaritas and listen to eclectic sets from the DJ. It's loads of fun. (📞02-6262 6968; www.drinkhonkytonks.com.au; 17 Garema Pl; 🕒3pm-late Mon-Thu, from noon Fri, from 2pm Sat)

Cube
GAY & LESBIAN

27 🕒 MAP P76, G6

Canberra's one and only gay club has been partying in this basement for practically forever. These days it seems to attract as many straight women as gay men. There are cheap drinks on Thirsty Thursdays; check the website for other events. (📞02-6257 1110; www. cubenightclub.com.au; 33 Petrie Plaza; 🕒10pm-late Thu-Sun)

Transit Bar
BAR

28 🕒 MAP P76, B3

Tucked under the YHA hostel, this bar hosts regular events including trivia, karaoke and live music. Look forward to a good range of Aussie craft beers. (☎02-6162 0899; www.facebook.com/transitbar; 7 Akuna St; ⏱noon-11pm Mon-Thu, to 1am Fri & Sat)

Entertainment

Dendy Canberra
CINEMA

29 ⭐ MAP P76, G5

An independent and art-house cinema in the Canberra Centre. Tuesday is discount day when all tickets are $13. (☎02-6221 8900; www.dendy.com.au; 2nd fl, Canberra Centre, 148 Bunda St; adult/child $19/14)

Canberra Theatre Centre
THEATRE

30 ⭐ MAP P76, B3

Canberra's live theatre hub hosts all kinds of performances, from theatre to cabaret to comedy. Check online to see what's playing during your visit, or pop into the box office. (☎02-6275 2700; www.canberratheatrecentre.com.au; London Circuit, Civic Sq; ⏱box office 9am-5pm Mon-Fri, 10am-2pm Sat)

Gorman Arts Centre
ARTS CENTRE

31 ⭐ MAP P76, D2

This sprawling arts centre – and its sister centre in Ainslie – plays host to a wide range of Canberra's cultural institutions, from galleries to theatre companies to individual artists. There's always something going on here, be it an exhibition, play, concert or multimedia interactive artwork; check the website to see what's happening during your visit. (☎02-6182 0000; www.agac.com.au; 55 Ainslie Ave, Braddon; ⏱hours vary)

Shopping

Craft ACT
HOMEWARES

32 🔒 MAP P76, B2

Part design shop, part museum, this beautiful space showcases art from local craftspeople and stages temporary exhibitions. (☎02-6262 9993; www.craftact.org.au; 1st fl, North Bldg, 180 London Circuit; ⏱10am-5pm Tue-Fri, noon-4pm Sat Feb-Dec)

Canberra Centre
MALL

33 🔒 MAP P76, C2

Sprawling over several city blocks, this vast shopping centre includes a multiscreen cinema, a food court and department stores, as well as design, fashion and homewares retailers. (☎02-6247 5611; www.canberracentre.com.au; Bunda St; ⏱9am-5.30pm Mon-Thu, to 9pm Fri, to 5pm Sat, 10am-4pm Sun)

Walking Tour 🥾

Stroll Around Lake Burley Griffin

The flat, paved path around Lake Burley Griffin is well-trafficked by locals who make good use of the circuit to walk their dogs, jog, cycle or just catch up with friends. There are sights along the way, but the most enjoyable part is just strolling by the lake shore in the fresh air.

Walk Facts

Start Teddy Picker's
End National Carillon
Length 5km; 1½ hours

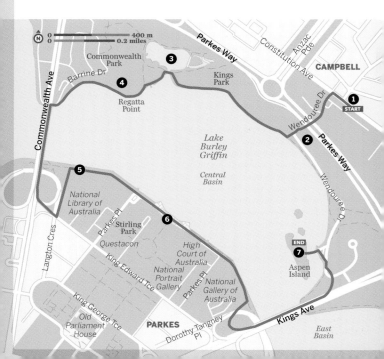

❶ Teddy Picker's

Fuel your walk with a coffee at this popular **brunch spot** (☎ 02-6230 1319; www.teddypickers.com.au; 65 Constitution Ave, Campbell; dishes $16-20; ⏰ 6.30am-3pm Mon-Fri, from 8am Sat & Sun; ❄) in Campbell, not far from the lakeshore. If you're peckish, the all-day menu has plenty to tempt taste buds.

❷ Blundell's Cottage

This small stone **worker's cottage** (www.nca.gov.au/attraction/blundells-cottage; Wendouree Dr, Campbell; admission free; ⏰ 10am-2pm Sat) was built in 1860, when the surrounding land was all farmland. It has been preserved in its original location as a physical reminder of Canberra's recent history. It has limited hours but if it's open, be sure to pop your head inside. Otherwise you can admire its stone exterior.

❸ Nerang Pool

As you stroll around the lakeside path, take a short detour to circle lovely **Nerang Pool** (Commonwealth Park). Surrounded by weeping willows and tall poplar trees, this peaceful pond is a haven for birds. The path around it takes in some lovely gardens and outdoor sculptures.

❹ National Capital Exhibition

Inside the Canberra & Region Visitors Centre, this small exhibition (p79) traces Canberra's history from the Ngunnawal people, Canberra's original Indigenous Australian residents, to construction of the national capital and the creation of Lake Burley Griffin.

❺ Australian of the Year Walk

After crossing Commonwealth Bridge, you'll stumble across this pathway lined with plinths commemorating each Australian of the Year. Running underneath the plinths, the five lines carved into the path represent the lines of a musical stave, with the plinths' placement corresponding with the notes of *Advance Australia Fair*.

❻ International Flag Display

As you walk along the lakeshore you'll see the National Library, Questacon, the National Portrait Gallery and the National Gallery of Australia in a line to your right, with Parliament House in the distance beyond. In front of Parliament House you'll find the **display** (Queen Elizabeth Tce) of international flags, one for every country with diplomatic representation in Canberra.

❼ National Carillon

Crossing back to the northern lakeshore you can see small Aspen Island, connected to King's Park by a curving pedestrian bridge. Atop the island, the striking National Carillon (p79) was gifted to Canberra by the British government in 1970 to celebrate the capital's 50th anniversary.

Explore ✦

Braddon

Hip Braddon is Canberra's latest shopping and dining precinct, with such a large concentration of excellent foodie options on its main Lonsdale St strip that you may never want to leave. The surrounding streets are home to a constantly increasing number of residential developments, meaning this is a great spot to get a taste of local Canberra life. There's not much in the way of tourist sights nearby, but you'll probably be too busy shopping and drinking cold-brew coffee to notice.

The Short List

○ **Kyō Coffee Project (p96)** *Starting your explorations off right with smooth, rich batch-brew coffee.*

○ **Rye (p93)** *Elevating your lunch to the next level with Danish smørrebrød open sandwiches at this sleek, welcoming cafe.*

○ **Lazy Su (p94)** *Noshing on Canberra's best Asian-inspired dishes at this hip local fave.*

○ **Bison Home (p98)** *Coveting a rainbow of locally designed bowls, plates and coffee mugs inside this gallery-esque homewares retailer.*

○ **Lonsdale St Traders (p99)** *Finding plenty of treasures to take home from the many petite shops inside this popular arcade.*

Getting There & Around

✈ Braddon's main strip is an easy stroll from the city centre.

🚌 Elouera St.

🚗 There's paid street parking (per hour from $3.10) along Lonsdale St, as well as a large parking lot at the top end near Girrahween St.

Neighbourhood Map on p92

Lonsdale Street 7 Roasters (p97) GEORGE FRANCIS DUNFORD/LONELY PLANET ©

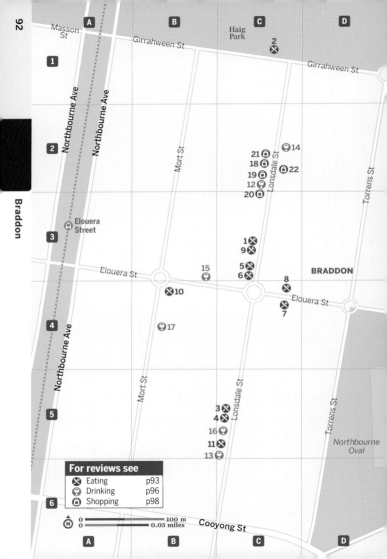

Braddon

Masson St

Girrahween St

Haig Park

Girrahween St

Northbourne Ave

Northbourne Ave

Mort St

Lonsdale St

Torrens St

2 ✕

21 🔒
18 🔒   🔒 14
19 🔒   🔒 22
12 🔒
20 🔒

Elouera
Street

1 ✕
9 ✕

Elouera St

15 🍷

5 ✕
6 ✕

BRADDON

8 ✕

✕ 10

Elouera St

7 ✕

Northbourne Ave

🍷 17

Mort St

Lonsdale St

3 ✕
4 ✕

Torrens St

16 🍷
11 ✕
13 🍷

Northbourne
Oval

For reviews see
✕ Eating   p93
🍷 Drinking   p96
🔒 Shopping   p98

N   0   100 m
     0   0.05 miles

Cooyong St

Eating

Messina
ICE CREAM $

1 ✕ MAP P92, C3

Sydney's favourite gelato maker has made it down the road to Braddon, where people queue to get their hands on the unique flavours – try combinations like pear and rhubarb, or salted caramel and mango salsa. Animal lovers rejoice: the sorbets are all vegan. (📞02-6152 0408; www.gelato messina.com; 4/21 Lonsdale St; ice cream from $5.30; ⏰noon-10.30pm Sun-Thu, to 11.30pm Fri & Sat; 🍴)

Mandalay
FOOD TRUCK $

2 ✕ MAP P92, C1

Canberrans know the best spot for a late-night bite is this big yellow bus, which sits in the car park at the top of Lonsdale St. There are no white tablecloths, just superb Burmese curry and waffle fries wolfed down atop milk crates. BYO drinks. (www.facebook.com/the mandalaybus; cnr Lonsdale & Girrawheen Sts, Braddon; dishes $7-10; ⏰6pm-late Wed-Sat)

Rye
CAFE $$

3 ✕ MAP P92, C5

Charming, Scandi-inspired Rye is all blonde wood, bright lights and modish furniture, with a menu to match. Danish *smørrebrød* (open sandwiches on dark rye bread) are a popular choice at lunch, while breakfast options are variations on cafe faves like poached eggs and avocado with Danish feta and broad beans.

Mandalay

Great coffee. (📞02-6156 9694; www.ryecafe.com.au; 9 Lonsdale St, Braddon; breakfast $14-17, lunch $7-22; ⏰6.30am-4pm)

Lazy Su

ASIAN $$

4 🍴 MAP P92, C5

Lazy Su's playful Asian vibe is obvious as you enter past the wall of lucky cats. You can't go far wrong with the menu, but if you can't decide between the pork-belly *baoger* and the yellowfin tuna tataki, opt for the seven-dish 'People's Banquet' ($49 per person).

If you're not hungry, prop up the bar and swig on a classic Japanese whisky or Korean *makgeolli*. Once a month it runs hip-hop and ramen nights, spinning old-school beats and serving ample bowls. (📞02-5105 3812; www.lazy-su.com.au; 9 Lonsdale St, Braddon; dishes $12-29; ⏰5-11pm Mon, from noon Tue-Thu & Sun, to 1am Fri & Sat)

Greasy Monkey

BURGERS $$

5 🍴 MAP P92, C3

Don't be put off by the name – the burgers here are fresh, juicy and delicious. Vegetarians will appreciate the portobello mushroom burger, while the sides are also lots of fun, including mozzarella sticks, jalapeño poppers and loaded cheesy fries. Happy hour is from 4pm to 6pm weekdays. (📞02-6174 1401; www.greasys.com.au; 19 Lonsdale St, Braddon; burgers $15-20; ⏰11am-late)

Elk & Pea

GEORGE FRANCIS DUNFORD/LONELY PLANET ©

Catch
FISH & CHIPS $$

6 MAP P92, C3

Catch takes regular fish and chips and turns up the dial. Choose from market-fresh hake, flathead, snapper, barramundi or salmon, battered or grilled, alongside a generous serving of hot, crispy chips. There's Capital Brewery ale on tap, as well as wine and cider. Take it away, or eat in bustling picnic tables set in an undercover Astro-turfed courtyard. (📞02-6247 2636; www.catchfishandchips.com.au; cnr Lonsdale & Elouera Sts; fish & chips $16-23; ⏱11am-late)

Sweet Bones
VEGAN $$

7 MAP P92, C4

Cruelty-free does not mean taste-free at this fully vegan cafe that crouches in a humble shopfront just off Lonsdale St. It does a mean all-day breakfast that could include a blueberry-pancake stack or coconut-water porridge. Its egg-free baking has scored awards for the likes of the almond and hazelnut brownie and cinnamon and sugar pretzels.

Bigger bellies can go for inventive burgers – add coconut bacon to marinated tofu for a flavour bigger than any meat. The Mexican menu runs to a huge burrito bowl, gluttonous nachos and other tasty treats. (📞0413 067 890; www.sweetbonescompany.com; Shop 8, 18 Lonsdale St, Braddon; mains $13-20; ⏱8am-4pm Mon-Sat, 8.30am-3pm Sun; 🌿)

Vegan Eats
🍽

It can be hard to find vegan options when you're in a new city, but Braddon has your back: not only is there an excellent vegan cafe, Sweet Bones, but one of the neighbourhood's best restaurants, Lazy Su, offers a full vegan banquet. For dessert hit up Messina (p93), where all the sorbets are vegan-friendly.

Eightysix
MODERN AUSTRALIAN $$

8 MAP P92, C4

Prepare to share at this zippy contemporary place, where dishes range from delectable steamed duck buns to a whole lamb shoulder. Solo travellers should opt to sit at the kitchen counter and watch the precision of the kitchen in full swing. If you're part of a visiting sumo-wrestling team or just a shameless food lover, order the $110 all-you-can-eat option. (📞02-6161 8686; www.eightysix.com.au; cnr Elouera & Lonsdale Sts; dishes $20-45)

Elk & Pea
LATIN AMERICAN $$

9 MAP P92, C3

Mexican influences pervade the menu and cocktail list of this cool little anytime place, which includes spicy eggs for brekkie, burgers and wraps for lunch, and Carribean jerk chicken for dinner. Be sure to try the fabulous cocktails, like

Coffee Heaven

Braddon is one of the best places in the city for caffeine addicts. Try longstanding local favourite Lonsdale Street 7 Roasters, or more recent up-starts Kyō Coffee Project and Barrio Collective Coffee.

the Tijuana Swizzle with tequila, Aperol, coconut water, passion fruit and rosé. (📞0436 355 732; www.elkandpea.com.au; 21 Lonsdale St; breakfast & lunch $11-25, tacos $8, shared plates $39-45; 🕑7am-late Tue-Sat, to 3pm Sun & Mon)

Les Bistronomes FRENCH $$$

10 🔀 MAP P92, B4

Wine bottles line the wall and the melodious French language radiates from the kitchen at this excellent little bistro. At $55, the five-course Saturday set lunch is terrific value; expect a succession of perfectly cooked, beautifully presented dishes that will leave you comfortably full without straining your belt. (📞02-6248 8119; www.lesbistronomes.net; cnr Mort & Elouera Sts, Braddon; mains $31-38; 🕑noon-2pm & 6-9pm Tue-Sat)

Italian & Sons ITALIAN $$$

11 🔀 MAP P92, C5

As Italian as can be, this stylish trattoria serves thin-crust pizza, phenomenal homemade pasta

and a single dish of the day to a loyal clientele – along with a good range of Italian wine to wash it down with. Book ahead. (📞02-6162 4888; www.italianandsons.com.au; 7 Lonsdale St; mains $24-38; 🕑noon-2pm & 6-10pm Tue-Fri, 6-10pm Mon & Sat)

Drinking

Kyō Coffee Project COFFEE

12 🚇 MAP P92, C2

In a little courtyard just off Lonsdale St, achingly hip Kyō serves coffee just as good as its slick, minimalist fit-out promises. Options are limited to black, white or a batch brew. There's a petite, mildly Japanese-inspired menu if you're peckish. (www.kyocoffee project.com; 5/27 Lonsdale St, Braddon; 🕑7am-4pm Tue-Sat, 7.30am-3.30pm Sun)

Hopscotch PUB

13 🚇 MAP P92, C5

An upmarket pub at the centre of Braddon's growing fine-dining strip. The front beer garden is the place to be on summer nights, where regular live-music performances add to the atmosphere. A good range of beers on tap, as well as notable whisky and wine lists, complete the picture. (📞02-6107 3030; www.hopscotch bar.com.au; 5 Lonsdale St, Braddon; 🕑11am-late)

Barrio Collective Coffee

COFFEE

14 😊 MAP P92, C2

Small but mighty, this wood-and-concrete space is a favourite with locals, who duck in at all times of day for a caffeine hit. The toasted sandwiches are also a winner. On Friday nights the space morphs into a lovely spot for a drink or two. (www.barriocollective.com; 59/30 Lonsdale St, Braddon; ⏱7am-2pm Mon-Fri, from 8am Sat & Sun, bar 5pm-late Fri)

BentSpoke Brewing Co

MICROBREWERY

15 😊 MAP P92, B3

With 16 excellent beers and ciders on tap, BentSpoke is one of Australia's best craft brewers. Sit at the bike-themed bar or relax outside and kick things off with a tasting tray of four beers ($16). Our favourite is the Barley Griffin Ale, subtly tinged with a spicy Belgian yeast. Good pub food, too.

These days you can get cans (featuring the tear-off top) of its beer in most local bottle shops, but it's still worth drinking the beverage where it is brewed and discovering a few surprises on tap. (☎02-6257 5220; www.bentspoke brewing.com.au; 38 Mort St, Braddon; ⏱11am-midnight)

Lonsdale Street 7 Roasters

COFFEE

16 😊 MAP P92, C5

In trendy Braddon, this grungy-chic cafe serves up damn fine

Lazy Su (p94)

GEORGE FRANCIS DUNFORD/LONELY PLANET ©

coffee along with tasty pastries and paninis. Head upstairs for a spacious, light-filled seating area with street views. (www.facebook.com/lonsdalestroasters; 7 Lonsdale St, Braddon; mains $9-12; ⏲6.30am-4pm Mon-Fri, from 8am Sat & Sun)

Knightsbridge Penthouse
COCKTAIL BAR

17 MAP P92, B4

Just behind the main Braddon strip, this quirky place offers good DJs, excellent cocktails and a mellow ambience. Come on Fridays before 8pm for 'Happy Friday' cheap cocktails ($10) and house wine ($5). (☎02-6262 6221; www.knightsbridgepenthouse.com.au; 34 Mort St, Braddon; ⏲5pm-midnight Tue & Wed, to late Thu-Sat)

Shopping

Bison Home
CERAMICS

18 MAP P92, C2

A Braddon outpost of Pialligo-based ceramics label Bison, this aesthetically pleasing shop will have you rethinking every object in your kitchen, from mugs to mixing bowls. Smaller items – like tiny ceramic milk bottles in a rainbow of colours – make lovely souvenirs or gifts. (☎02-6128 0788; www.bisonhome.com; 14/27 Lonsdale St, Braddon; ⏲10am-5pm Mon-Fri, to 4pm Sat & Sun)

Kin Gallery
JEWELLERY

19 MAP P92, C2

This beautiful space is a gallery, shop and workshop all rolled into

Sweet Bones (p95)

GEORGE FRANCIS DUNFORD/LONELY PLANET ©

one. Browse beautiful jewellery from more than 60 Australian designers and find something sparkly to take home with you. For a more unique gift, book a class on making your own wedding rings – by appointment only. (📞0431 052 214; www.kin.gallery; 6/27 Lonsdale St; 🕙10am-5.30pm Tue-Fri, to 4pm Sat, 11am-3pm Sun)

Lost Vintage

CLOTHING

20 🔒 MAP P92, C3

A carefully curated selection of vintage fashion is on offer at this tiny shop, tucked away at the back of the small retail space at 27 Lonsdale. If you're feeling a bit dowdy strolling around supercool Braddon, this is the place to find some proper cool duds. (www.facebook.com/lostvintagecbr; 3a/27 Lonsdale St; 🕙11am-5.30pm Wed-Fri, to 4pm Sat & Sun)

Bitten Goodfoods

FOOD & DRINKS

21 🔒 MAP P92, C2

Pick up superlative picnicking supplies at this eco-conscious grocer and food store, which also offers excellent prepared meals and green smoothies. (www.bitten goodfoods.com; 17/27 Lonsdale St; 🕙7am-8pm Mon-Fri, 8am-6pm Sat, 9am-5pm Sun)

Lonsdale St Traders

MALL

22 🔒 MAP P92, C2

Find homewares, fashion, jewellery and other lovely things to covet at this small collection of stores in the heart of Braddon. (www.facebook.com/lonsdalestreettraders; 30 Lonsdale St; 🕙store hours vary)

Explore ✦
Dickson & the North

Canberra's sprawling northern suburbs are largely residential, with wide leafy streets interspersed by plenty of parks and bushland. Residents congregate around smaller suburban hubs for shopping and dining, all of which have a distinctive character. The bustling centre of Dickson is Canberra's Asian quarter, with Korean, Thai, Vietnamese, Chinese, Japanese and Malaysian restaurants all jostling for patrons. Smaller village satellites such as Ainslie and Lyneham are also home to some culinary gems and make good excursions.

The Short List

○ **Capital Region Farmers Market (p109)** Perusing picnic supplies and nibbling local nosh at the oldest and largest of Canberra's farmers markets.

○ **Highroad (p104)** Dining on interesting, seasonal dishes, from breakfast through to dinner at Dickson locals' new favourite cafe.

○ **Pilot (p107)** Experiencing unique flavour combinations, impeccable service and excellent drink pairings at this fine-dining gem in suburban Ainslie.

○ **Old Canberra Inn (p107)** Sipping craft beers and bopping to live music in the sunny courtyard at Canberra's oldest pub.

Getting There & Around
🚌 Macarthur Ave or Dickson Interchange.

🚌 Route 31 or 53.

🚗 There's plenty of parking in Dickson, Ainslie and Lyneham.

Neighbourhood Map on p102

Mt Ainslie (p104) DAVID WALL/ALAMY STOCK ©

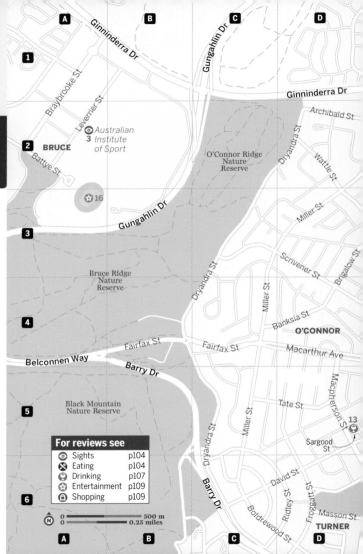

For reviews see

0 ————— 500 m
0 ————— 0.25 miles

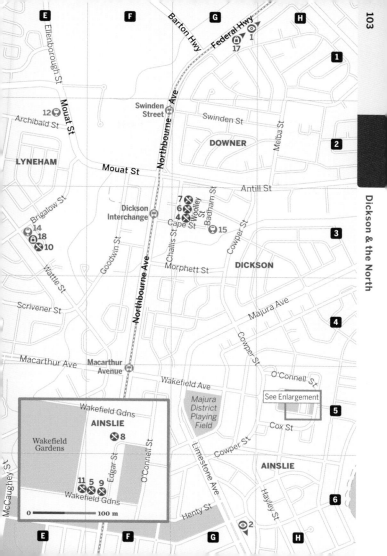

E
F
G
H

Barton Hwy

Federal Hwy

1

17

1

Ellenborough St

Swinden
Street

Swinden St

Melba St

DOWNER

2

12

Mouat St

Archibald St

Northbourne Ave

LYNEHAM

Mouat St

Antill St

3

Brigalow St

Dickson
Interchange

7

6

Woolley

Wolley

4

Cape St

Badham St

Cowper St

15

14

18

10

Goodwin St

Challis St

Morphett St

DICKSON

Wattle St

Scrivener St

Majura Ave

Cowper St

4

Macarthur Ave

Macarthur
Avenue

Northbourne Ave

O'Connell St

5

Wakefield Ave

See Enlargement

Majura
District
Playing
Field

Cox St

Wakefield Gdns

AINSLIE

Wakefield
Gardens

8

Edgar St

O'Connell St

Cowper St

AINSLIE

11 5 9

Wakefield Gdns

McCaughey St

Henty St

Limestone Ave

Hayley St

6

0 —————— 100 m

2

E
F
G
H

Sights

Mt Majura   NATURE RESERVE

1 ⊙ MAP P102, G1

In the city's northeast corner, behind Mt Ainslie, Mt Majura (888m) offers wonderful views from the lookout at its summit and splendid bushwalking opportunities. The Casuarina Trail (departing from Antill St in Dickson) is a lovely two-hour (3.8km) walk that tramps through the bush and along the ridge. See the website for a map. (www.majura.org; Mt Majura Rd)

Mt Ainslie   NATURE RESERVE

2 ⊙ MAP P102, G6

Northeast of the city, 843m-high Mt Ainslie has excellent views day and night. At the top, plaques explain what the Canberra basin looked like before the city was built. You can drive to the summit, or take the walking track that starts behind the Australian War Memorial (p74; 4.5km return, 1½ hours). (www.environment.act.gov.au/parks-conservation/parks-and-reserves; Ainslie Dr)

Australian Institute of Sport   SCHOOL

3 ⊙ MAP P102, A2

The country's elite and aspiring athletes hone their sporting prowess at the AIS. Visitors can take 90-minute guided tours of the facilities, led by resident athletes. There are also displays on Australian champions, plus interactive exhibits where you can publicly humble yourself at a variety of sports or test the accuracy, speed and strength of your ball skills and reaction time. (AIS; ☑02-6214 1010; www.experienceais.com; Leverrier St, Bruce; adult/child $20/12; ⊙tours 10am, 11.30am, 1pm & 2.30pm)

Eating

Highroad   CAFE $$

4 MAP P102, G3

Opened in 2017, Highroad has quickly found its groove. Locals fill the tables in the spacious corner building from lunch to dinner, supping on speciality-blend coffee in the mornings and local wines as the sun sets. The menu spans the gamut of Mod Oz cafe fare, from French toast to burgers, with a focus on local and seasonal ingredients. (www.highrd.com.au; cnr Cape

---

Bushwalking Capital

Dickson and Canberra's northern suburbs are mostly residential, with not much in the way of traditional tourist sights. Both Mt Ainslie, to the east, and Mt Majura, further north, are home to plenty of hiking and bushwalking opportunities, and offer great views from lookouts at their summits.

STEVEN TRITTON/SHUTTERSTOCK ©

Australian Institute of Sport

& Woolley Sts, Dickson; brunch $11-24, dinner $16-30; ⊙7am-4pm Mon-Wed, to late Fri, 8am-late Sat, to 3pm Sun)

Mama Dough
PIZZA $$

5 MAP P102, F6

These folks do fabulous takeaway pizzas, but if the weather is nice an even better option is to nab a seat under the fairy lights at the handful of outdoor tables (there's no indoor seating). Options range from the 'usuals' (Margherita, hot salami) to the 'unusuals' (bolognese and ricotta or zucchini and speck). Save room for a Nutella calzone for dessert. (☑02-6248 0591; www.mamadough.com.au; 2 Wakefield Gardens, Ainslie; pizzas $19-25; ⊙5pm-late)

Asian Noodle House
ASIAN $$

6 MAP P102, G3

A Canberra institution, Dickson's Noodle House is consistently chock-a-block full of converts slurping up its renowned laksa. The decor's nothing to write home about, but never mind: you're here for the food. If laksa is not your thing there are plenty of other options available, with the menu spanning Malaysian, Thai and Lao cuisine. Credit cards are not accepted. (☑02-6247 6380; www. noodlehouse.net.au; 29 Woolley St, Dickson; mains $14-20; ⊙11am-9pm Tue-Sun)

Au Lac

VEGAN $$

7 MAP P102, G3

Herbivores rejoice: this excellent vegan restaurant has your Asian-food cravings sorted, from stir-fries to laksas to rice-paper rolls. Most dishes use soy-based meat-alternatives – either regular tofu or soy 'fish', 'chicken' and 'beef'. Banquets (from $30 per person, minimum four people) are also available. (02-6262 8922; www.aulac-restaurant.com.au; 4/35-39 Woolley St; mains $14-19; 11.30am-2.30pm & 5.30-10.30pm Tue-Sun, 5.30-10.30pm Mon;)

Breizh

FRENCH $$

8 MAP P102, F5

A traditional French crêperie might seem out of place in suburban Canberra, but this place is the real deal. Stop by for a crepe (sweet) or galette (savoury), alongside a *bolée* (bowl) of apple cider. And don't neglect the *pâtisseries* (pastries) – they're absolutely to die for. (02-6156 0346; www.breizhcafecreperie.com; 2/15 Edgar St, Ainslie; dishes $7-20; 9am-4pm Wed-Sat, to 3pm Sun)

Edgar's Inn

PUB FOOD $$

9 MAP P102, F6

From breakfast right through to last drinks, this friendly corner pub in Ainslie bustles with locals. Changing weekday specials (like a burger and drink for $18) draw the crowds, but the food is great whatever the occasion. (02-6257

Edgar's Inn

STEVEN TRITTON/SHUTTERSTOCK ©

5488; 1 Edgar St, Ainslie; mains $14-25; ⏰7am-late Mon-Fri, from 8am Sat & Sun)

Front

CAFE $$

10 ✖ MAP P102, E3

Part art gallery, part cafe, the Front has a minimalist, aesthetic vibe. The brunch menu is short and sweet, with unique options like a radish, mint and beetroot breakfast bowl, or ricotta hotcakes with elderflower yoghurt. The same clever touches are on show at dinner, when they're accompanied by a well-curated wine list. (www.frontgallerycafe.com; 2 Wattle St, Lyneham; dishes $12-20; ⏰7am-3pm Tue, to late Wed-Fri, 8am-late Sat, to 3pm Sun)

Pilot

MODERN AUSTRALIAN $$$

11 ✖ MAP P102, E6

Elegant, seasonal dishes are the highlight at this classy fine-dining restaurant in suburban Ainslie. The menu changes daily but features local produce and interesting flavour combinations. À la carte options are available, but for the full experience try the 'prix fixe' tasting menu, available paired with either alcoholic or nonalcoholic beverages. There's also a Sunday 'long lunch' for $60 per person. (☎02-6257 4334; www.pilotrestaurant.com; 5/6 Wakefield Gardens, Ainslie; mains $25-45; set menu per person $90, with paired drinks nonalcoholic/alcoholic $120/150; ⏰6pm-late Wed-Sat, noon-3.30pm Sun)

Vertical Parkrun

Every Saturday at 8am athletic types tackle the 5km Mt Ainslie (p104) summit track as part of Parkrun. Register for free at www.parkrun.com.au/mountainslie to join in the fun and have your time recorded.

Drinking

Old Canberra Inn

PUB

12 🍺 MAP P102, E2

Coming and going a few times over the last 160 years, Canberra's oldest pub is once again thriving. Today it pours a changing roster of craft beers in sprawling beer gardens with live music most weekends. In winter there's a crackling fire and several snug spots. The pub grub – including parmas and burgers, with handcut chips – is better than most. (☎02-6134 6000; www.oldcanberra inn.com.au; 196 Mouat St, Lyneham; ⏰11.30am-10pm Sun-Thu, to late Fri & Sat)

Duxton

PUB

13 🍺 MAP P102, D5

A surprisingly swish-looking pub with a wide range of beers on tap, including many local brews. The food can be hit and miss. Head upstairs for slightly less bustle.

(📞02-6162 0799; www.theduxton.
com.au; cnr Sargood & Macpherson
Sts, O'Connor; 🕐noon-late Mon-Thu,
from 11.30am Fri, from 9am Sat & Sun)

Tilley's Devine Cafe Gallery
BAR

14 🚇 MAP P102, E3

People of all ages breeze in and out
of Tilley's old-fashioned, darkened
interior, with its scuffed furniture,
dusky mirror glass and eclectic
roster of local and international
musicians and comedians. It
also does poetry nights, writers'
sessions and cooked breakfasts.
(📞02-6247 7753; www.tilleys.com.au;
cnr Wattle & Brigalow Sts, Lyneham;
🕐7.30am-late Mon-Sat, from 8am
Sun)

Canberra Wine House
WINE BAR

15 🚇 MAP P102, G3

Hidden inside the Tradies complex
(enter via the Quality Hotel recep-
tion) you'll find this small, sleek
wine bar that feels more Brooklyn
than Dickson. All the wines on offer
are from the Canberra region, with
a rotating selection available by
the glass, as well as various tasting
flights. Small nibbles – cheese
boards, dips and the like – are also
available.

For added quirk factor, sup your
drink inside the restored tram-
car that sits in the bar's indoor
courtyard. (📞02-6162 5649; www.
thecanberrawinehouse.com.au; 2
Badham St; 🕐4-9pm Wed-Thu, 3-10pm
Fri & Sat)

Capital Region Farmers Market

Entertainment

GIO Stadium
Canberra   STADIUM

16 ⭐ MAP P102, A3

The Canberra Raiders (www.raid-ers.com.au) is the hometown rugby league side, and in season (from March to September) the team plays here regularly. Also laying tackles here is the ACT Brumbies (www.brumbies.com.au) rugby union team, which plays in the international Super Rugby competition running February to August. (📞02-6256 6700; www.giostadiumcan-berra.com.au; Battye St, Bruce)

Shopping

Capital Region
Farmers Market   MARKET

17 🔲 MAP P102, G1

Stallholders from all over the surrounding region congregate every week at this excellent farmers market, which brings the best of the countryside into the reach of suburban Canberrans. Pick up farm-fresh produce, jams, chees-es, charcuterie, baked goods and more – plan to have breakfast (or an early lunch) at one of the many excellent food and drink stalls in the market. (www.capitalregion farmersmarket.com.au; Exhibition Park, off Federal Hwy, Mitchell; 🕐7.30am-noon Sat)

Book Lore   BOOKS

18 🔲 MAP P102, E3

This place is just what a second-hand bookshop should be, with shelves stacked to bursting with dusty volumes begging to be discovered by you. (📞02-6247 6450; 94 Wattle St, Lyneham; 🕐10am-5.30pm)

Walking Tour 🥾

Hall Village Walk

Pretty Hall, founded in 1882, maintains a village feel despite being within Canberra city limits. Just off the Barton Hwy, it makes a lovely stopover on the way to the Canberra wine region. The compact main street has several excellent shops and cafes, while a section of the Canberra Centenary Trail is a good interlude for energetic types.

Getting There

🚗 Hall is a 30-minute (17km) drive from central Canberra on the Barton Hwy (A25).

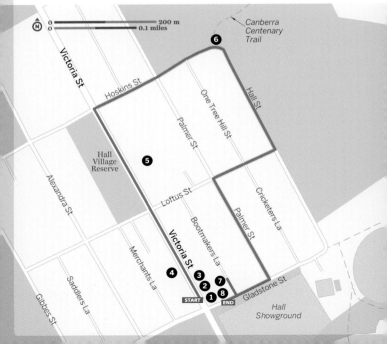

❶ Kynefin

Start with breakfast at **Kynefin** (☎02-6230 9777; 2 Victoria St; dishes $12-18; ☉7am-4pm Wed-Sat, from 8am Sun, kitchen closes 2pm; P ❄), a lovely modern cafe that feels more like an urban coffee shop than a country diner. Mornings see locals filling outside tables to sip excellent coffee and devour fresh, seasonal breakfasts – we like the simple granola, topped with whatever fruit is in season.

❷ Beatrix & Bertram

Tiny **Beatrix & Bertram** (☎02-6230 2829; 4 Victoria St; ☉7.30am-5pm Mon-Fri) is tucked inside the village post office, and has a lovely curated selection of homewares, women's fashion and accessories that are definitely worth a browse.

❸ Hops & Vine

If you won't make it to the Canberra wine region, don't worry: this excellent **beer and wine purveyor** (☎02-6230 2862; 6a Victoria St; ☉11am-7pm Wed-Sat, to 5pm Sun) has you covered. Grab a bottle or two of excellent local vintages under the expert tutelage of the friendly staff, who really know their pinot from their prosecco.

❹ Daughters at Hall

Stop for coffee and cake at this **converted general store** (☎02-6230 2457; 5 Victoria St; breakfasts $7-21, cakes $4-7; ☉6.30am-5.30pm Mon-Fri, 8am-4pm Sat & Sun), which now operates as a friendly cafe. While you're there, peruse homemade jams and other local produce by the counter, and pick up something for later.

❺ Hall School Museum

This petite local history **museum** (24 Victoria St; admission free; ☉9am-noon Thu, noon-4pm Sun) is run by a group of committed residents. It has limited opening hours but if it's open during your visit then definitely poke your nose inside to get a sense of Hall's historical past.

❻ One Tree Hill Lookout

If you're feeling energetic, an easily accessible section of Canberra's 145km Centenary Trail departs from Hall's northern end. The hike to One Tree Hill is 8.5km (two hours) return, so you'll definitely have earned your lunch by the time you get back.

❼ Capital Wines

You don't need to trek to Murrumbateman to taste local produce: **Capital Wines' cellar door** (☎02-6230 2022; 13 Gladstone St; ☉10.30am-5pm Thu-Sun) is right in the centre of Hall. Drop in to try some of their superb vintages; the acclaimed 'ministry series' wines come well recommended.

❽ 1882

End your visit with a long lunch at **1882** (☎02-6230 2113; 13 Gladstone St; mains $25-35; ☉11.30am-10pm Tue-Thu, to 11pm Fri, from 8am Sat, to 10pm Sun), a charming local pub that is a big hit with locals.

Explore ✪ Kingston & Manuka

Southeast of Capital Hill, the residential suburbs of Kingston and Manuka are well known for being culinary hotspots, with more than their fair share of drinking and dining options. The old village of Kingston still has plenty to keep visitors interested, while new restaurants and cafes are popping up all the time along the developing foreshore precinct. In nearby Manuka (pronounced Maa-neka, not Ma-nu-ka), residents congregate around a tree-lined square where there are several charming places to while away the hours.

The Short List

∘ **Old Bus Depot Markets (p121)** *Perusing crafts and fresh produce while noshing down on international cuisine at this Canberra institution.*

∘ **GoBoat (p116)** *Becoming captain of your own small vessel to cruise the less-discovered corners of Lake Burley Griffin, picnic in tow.*

∘ **Silo Bakery (p118)** *Picking up some of Canberra's most delicious baked goods for a lakeside picnic.*

∘ **Muse (p117)** *Dining on fabulous seasonal cuisine and fabulous coffee before heading downstairs for a post-prandial browse of the well-curated bookshop.*

Getting There & Around
🚌 Routes 56, R6 or R2.

🚗 There's plenty of on-street parking around.

🚶 If you're staying in Barton, it's a short walk to Kingston.

Neighbourhood Map on p114

Kingston foreshore DANIJELC/GETTY IMAGES ©

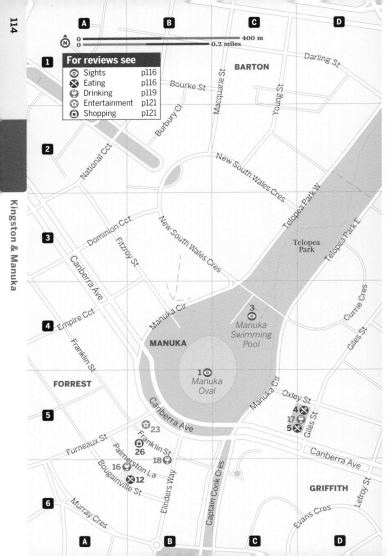

Kingston & Manuka

For reviews see

⊙	Sights	p116
✕	Eating	p116
🍷	Drinking	p119
★	Entertainment	p121
🔒	Shopping	p121

0   400 m
0   0.2 miles

BARTON

Darling St

Bourke St

Macquarie St

Young St

Burbury Cl

National Cct

New South Wales Cres

Telopea Park W

Telopea Park E

Dominion Cct

Fitzroy St

New South Wales Cres

Telopea Park

Canberra Ave

Currie Cres

Empire Cct

Manuka Cir

Giles St

MANUKA

3 ⊙
Manuka
Swimming
Pool

Franklin St

1 ⊙
Manuka
Oval

FORREST

Canberra Ave

Manuka Cir

Oxley St

4 ✕
17 ✕
5 ✕

Giles St

23 ★

Furneaux St

Franklin St

26 🔒

Palmerston La

18 🍷

Canberra Ave

Elinders Way

16 🔒

Bougainville St

12 ✕

GRIFFITH

Murray Cres

Captain Cook Cres

Evans Cres

Letroy Cres

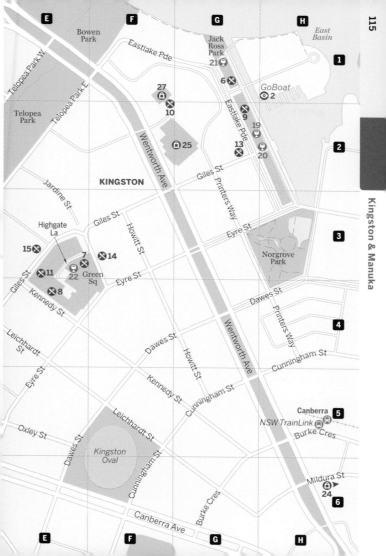

E
F
G
H

1
2
3
4
5
6

Bowen Park

Eastlake Pde

Jack Ross Park

East Basin

21

6

GoBoat 2

27

10

9

19

20

25

13

Telopea Park W

Telopea Park E

Telopea Park

Wentworth Ave

KINGSTON

Giles St

Printers Way

Eyre St

Jardine St

Giles St

Howitt St

Norgrove Park

Highgate La

15

7

14

11

22

Green Sq

8

Eyre St

Kennedy St

Giles St

Dawes St

Printers Way

Leichhardt St

Dawes St

Howitt St

Wentworth Ave

Cunningham St

Eyre St

Kennedy St

Cunningham St

Leichhardt St

Canberra 5

NSW TrainLink

Burke Cres

Oxley St

Dawes St

Kingston Oval

Cunningham St

Mildura St

24

Canberra Ave

Burke Cres

Sights

Manuka Oval   SPORTS GROUND

1 ◎ MAP P114, B5

This popular local sports stadium was inaugurated in the 1920s and now plays host to AFL and cricket matches, including its first game of International test cricket in 2019. (02-6228 0304; www. manukaoval.com.au; Manuka Circle, Griffith)

GoBoat   BOATING

2 ◎ MAP P114, H1

Fancy pottering around Lake Burley Griffin on your own private boat? These little electric-powered dinghies can fit up to eight people and have a table in the centre just made for picnicking. You don't need a boat licence to captain your own cruise, just a sense of adventure. Bookings (via the website) are recommended. (02-6100 7776; www.goboatcanberra.com. au; Wharf 2, Trevillian Quay, Kingston Foreshore; 1/2/3hr $95/169/239; ⏲10am-8pm)

Manuka Swimming Pool   SWIMMING

3 ◎ MAP P114, C4

Escape the summer heat at Manuka's art-deco outdoor pool, which has a 30m lap pool as well as a shaded toddler wading pool and playground. (02-6295 1910; www.manukapool.com.au; NSW Cres, Griffith; adult/child $7/5; ⏲6.30am-7pm Mon-Fri, from 8am Sat & Sun Oct-Mar)

Eating

Agostini's   ITALIAN $$

4 ✕ MAP P114, D5

Wood-fired pizza, rosé on tap and house-made gelato are just some of the charms of this cool, millennial-pink bistro, set in the ground floor of East Hotel. Holidaying families rub shoulders with Canberra's glitterati along the plush, window seating; for a real show, however, request a seat at the bar with a view of the pizza oven. Reservations recommended. (02-6178 0048; www.easthotel.com.au/agositinis; 69

International Cricket

The intimate Manuka Oval seats only 13,500 people, but this hasn't stopped it attracting world-class sporting events. The oval hosts an annual match between the Prime Minister's XI cricket team and an international touring team, and in January 2019 held its first International Test between Australia and Sri Lanka, with more international matches planned for the future. Check the website for details.

Muse

Canberra Ave, Kingston; pizzas $21-25, mains from $25; ⊙noon-3pm & 5.30pm-late)

Muse
AUSTRALIAN $$

5 🗙 MAP P114, D5

This bibliophile restaurant-bookshop on the corner of the East Hotel effortlessly juggles its roles. Start with a drink from the Australian-only drinks list then move on to the 'prologues', including seasonal delights such as kingfish sashimi. Larger 'chapter' dishes include a generous sharing plate of spanner crab with garlic chips. Downstairs, a well-curated bookshop makes for a charming post-meal browse. Muse hosts a variety of events, including literary lunches and regular talks with the country's biggest authors. Like any good page-turner, you'll find it hard to tear yourself away. (📞02-6178 0024; www.musecanberra.com.au; 69 Canberra Ave, Kingston; mains breakfast $8-25, lunch $16-38, dinner $24-38; ⊙6.30am-3pm Mon-Tue, to 10pm Wed-Fri, 7am-10pm Sat, 7am-noon Sun)

Morks
THAI $$

6 🗙 MAP P114, G1

One of our favourite restaurants on the Kingston foreshore, Morks offers a contemporary spin on Thai cuisine, with Chinese and Malay elements added to the mix. Ask for a table outside to watch the passing promenade, and tuck into multiple serves of the starters; the sweet-potato dumplings in Penang curry are staggeringly good. (📞02-6295 0112; www.morks.com.au; 19

Eastlake Pde, Kingston; mains $18-44; ⊙noon-2pm & 6-10pm Wed-Fri & Sun, 6-10pm Tue & Sat)

Highgate House PUB FOOD $$

7 ✖ MAP P114, E3

Fronting onto Green Sq, this place offers decent pub meals in a light-filled, convivial environment. Mains can be a touch overpriced, but weekday dinner deals (like Tuesday's $20 steak and a drink) are good value. (☑02-6239 6891; www.highgatebar.com.au; Green Sq, 44 Jardine St, Kingston; mains $19-28; ⊙noon-late Tue-Sat, to 9pm Sun)

Penny University CAFE $$

8 ✖ MAP P114, E4

Bustling Penny University is packed all weekend long with Kingston locals who know exactly where to come for hearty meals and a linger-longer atmosphere. Standard breakfast items are given a twist with additions like miso-baked salmon, while fresh, seasonal produce features in lunchtime dishes from poke bowls to gnocchi. (☑02-6162 1500; www.pennyuniversitycafe. com; 15 Kennedy St, Kingston; dishes $8.50-27; ⊙7am-4pm)

Bad Betti's BURGERS $$

9 ✖ MAP P114, G2

Pumpin' tunes, fairy lights and AstroTurf set the tone at this casual lakeside burger bar. Come for the waterfront views and stay for the juicy burgers and tasty

sides, such as sweet-potato fries and avo-laden nachos. (☑02-6295 7000; 6/2 Trevillian Quay, Kingston Foreshore; burgers $16-18; ⊙noon-10pm Sun-Thu, to midnight Fri & Sat)

Brodburger BURGERS $$

10 ✖ MAP P114, F2

Brodburger started as a lakeside caravan takeaway joint. Now it has a permanent location, but the flame-grilled burgers are as good as ever. Not only is there a good range of meat, fish and vegetarian options, but you even get to pick from four types of cheese for the cheeseburger. (☑02-6162 0793; www.brodburger.com.au; Glassworks Bldg, 11 Wentworth Ave, Kingston; burgers $14-21; ⊙noon-3pm & 5.30pm-late Tue-Sat, noon-4pm Sun; 🖈)

Silo Bakery BAKERY, CAFE $$

11 ✖ MAP P114, E3

Top-class sourdough bread, pastries and tarts are perfect breakfast temptations, while an interesting menu of cooked dishes keeps diners happy at lunch. Good coffee and wines by the glass complete the package. Book ahead for lunch. (☑02-6260 6060; www.silobakery.com.au; 36 Giles St, Kingston; mains breakfast $9-20, lunch $18-27; ⊙7am-4pm Tue-Sat)

Urban Pantry CAFE $$

12 ✖ MAP P114, B6

This popular brunch spot boasts a chic bistro atmosphere inside and sunny tables in the small square outside. Unfortunately service can be a bit chaotic and dishes don't always live up to the menu's promises. (☎02-6162 3556; www.urbanpantrymanuka.com.au; 5 Bougainville St, Griffith; mains breakfast $15-19, lunch $21-32; ⏱7am-5.30pm Mon-Sat, to 4pm Sun; 🗲)

Wild Duck   SOUTHEAST ASIAN $$$

13 ❌ MAP P114, G2

Known as a favourite haunt of parliamentarians, this discreet restaurant impresses for its cuisine and its clientele. Try slow-cooked pork baked in lotus leaves or Massaman beef cheek – a Thai-inspired treat that ingeniously balances flavour and spice. The wine list is strong if traditional, with a Grange and Chateauneuf-Du-Pape. Vegetarian options are limited. (☎02-6232 7997; www.wild-duck.com.au; 77-78/71 Giles St, Kingston; mains $27-35, banquets per person $49-99; ⏱noon-2.30pm & 5.30pm-late Mon-Fri, 5.30pm-late Sat)

Otis   MODERN AUSTRALIAN $$$

14 ❌ MAP P114, F3

Sophisticated, Mod Oz cuisine is the centrepiece at Otis, with dishes such as salted wallaby with vine leaves and macadamias, or roast lamb with celeriac and buckwheat. An elegant ambience, excellent local wine list and killer cocktails round out the experience. Desserts are playful takes on Australian favourites – try the signature lemon-meringue 'magnum'. (☎02-6260 6066; www.thisisotis.com.au; 29

Jardine St, Kingston; mains from $32; ⏱noon-3pm & 5.30pm-late Tue-Sat)

Pomegranate   MEDITERRANEAN $$$

15 ❌ MAP P114, E3

Techniques from France combine with the traditions of the eastern Mediterranean, adding finesse to rustic dishes that burst with flavour. Despite the white-linen ambience, the serves are generous and the service is friendly and relaxed. (☎02-6295 1515; www.pomegranatekingston.com; 31 Giles St, Kingston; mains $19-36; ⏱noon-2pm & 6pm-late Tue-Sat)

Drinking

Ona   COFFEE

16 ☕ MAP P114, A6

Locally owned and roasted Ona coffee beans are the drawcard at this excellent cafe on the pedestrian mall in Manuka. Coffee-lovers should make a beeline for the sweet, perfectly brewed filter options. The dining choices are equally superlative. (www.onacoffee.com.au; Shop 4, the Lawns, Manuka; ⏱7am-4pm Mon-Fri, 8am-3pm Sat & Sun)

Joe's Bar   COCKTAIL BAR

17 ☕ MAP P114, D5

Colourful glass and draped metal beads add to the glitzy boho ambience at this attractive Italian wine bar attached to the East Hotel (p116). The extensive cocktail list includes a whole page of speciality gin and tonics, and the bar staff really know their Italian wines, too. Pace yourself with a serve of polenta chips, arancini balls or antipasti. (📞02-6178 0050; www. joesateast.com; 69 Canberra Ave, Kingston; ⏰4pm-late Tue-Sat)

Public Bar
PUB

18 🚇 MAP P114, B6

Hanging ferns and potted plants make this airy corner pub feel more oasis-like than its busy Manuka location would suggest. Street-side tables brim with locals on weekends; stop for a drink on your way to dinner, or linger longer for decent pub meals and pizzas. (📞02-6161 8808; 1-33 Flinders Way, Griffith; ⏰10am-late Mon-Fri, from 9am Sat & Sun)

Local Press
COFFEE

19 🚇 MAP P114, G2

Fabulous coffee is just the beginning at this lush foreshore cafe. Hanging plants and nautical decor bring the outside in, while fabulous veggie-heavy breakfasts and water views keep the locals coming. Be prepared to wait on weekends.

(📞02-6162 1422; www.local-press. com.au; 35 Eastlake Pde, Kingston; ⏰7am-3pm Mon-Fri, 8am-5pm Sat & Sun)

Dock
PUB

20 🚇 MAP P114, H2

This popular foreshore pub is packed to the brim with locals during happy hour (5pm to 6pm Monday to Thursday). There's a big screen for sports fans and live music most weekends. (📞02-6239 6333; www.thedockkingston.com.au; 7/81 Giles St, Kingston; ⏰11am-late)

Walt & Burley
PUB

21 🚇 MAP P114, G1

At the northern tip of the Kingston foreshore precinct, this cosy pub is a popular spot for an afternoon drink. The wood-burning fireplace is a hit in winter, while in the warmer months outdoor tables overlooking Lake Burley Griffin are the pick. The food menu promises a lot but sometimes fails to deliver. (📞02-6239 6648; www.waltandburley. com.au; 70/17 Eastlake Pde, Kingston; ⏰11am-late)

Glassmaking Classes

Creative types can get hands-on at the Canberra Glassworks, with regular classes offering beginners the opportunity to try their hand at glassblowing in the on-site 'hot shop'. Make your own paperweight, bird, drinking glass or vase while learning about the art of glassmaking inside this charming heritage building. Classes range from $85 to $130 per person; reserve in advance via the website.

Durham Castle Arms PUB

22 MAP P114, E3

A cosy village-pub wannabe in the middle of cafe-filled Kingston, the Durham is known for its craft beer, competitive Tuesday-night quiz and live music. (☏02-6295 1769; www.thedurhampub.com.au; Green Sq, Jardine St, Kingston; ☀noon-late)

Entertainment

Capitol Cinemas CINEMA

23 MAP P114, B5

Six-screen art-deco cinema screening mostly current block-busters. (☏02-6295 9042; www.eventcinemas.com.au; 6 Franklin St, Griffin; tickets $10)

Shopping

Fyshwick Fresh Food Markets MARKET

24 MAP P114, H6

The best place in Canberra to pick up fresh fruit and vegetables as well as all other kinds of gourmet goodies, from cheeses and char-cuteries to breads and pastries. (☏02-6295 0606; www.fyshwick markets.com.au; 36 Mildura St, Fysh-wick; ☀7am-5.30pm Thu-Sun)

Old Bus Depot Markets MARKET

25 MAP P114, G2

A Sunday institution, this bustling market has one hall completely devoted to food and another to crafts. Self-caterers and picnickers will delight in the freshly baked goods, cheese, charcuterie and produce; come at lunch to take full advantage of the 'international' food court, with cuisine from Thailand, Ethiopia, Jordan and the USA, as well as the usual pancakes and coffee. (☏02-6295 3331; www.obdm.com.au; 21 Wentworth Ave, Kingston; ☀10am-4pm Sun)

Paperchain BOOKS

26 MAP P114, B5

Fabulous independent bookstore with an excellent range of titles and friendly staff. (☏02-6295 6723; www.paperchainbookstore.com.au; 34 Franklin St, Manuka; ☀9am-8pm Sun-Thu, to 9pm Fri & Sat)

Canberra Glassworks ARTS & CRAFTS

27 MAP P114, F1

Call in to this converted Edward-ian power station, the young city's oldest public heritage building, to watch glass being blown in the 'hot shop' and to peruse the exquisite results in the adjacent gallery and shop. (☏02-6260 7005; www.canberraglassworks.com; 11 Wentworth Ave, Kingston; ☀10am-4pm Wed-Sun)

Walking Tour 🥾

Culinary Fyshwick

Industrial Fyshwick is not known as a tourist draw, but among its car yards, warehouses and superstores you'll find a plethora of hidden gems, including fabulous culinary hotspots, locally brewed beer and even bird-filled wetlands. The area can be brash and a bit dusty, but if you know where to look there's plenty to keep you occupied on this three-hour walk.

Getting There

🚌 Route 80 from the City Bus Station stops right outside the markets.

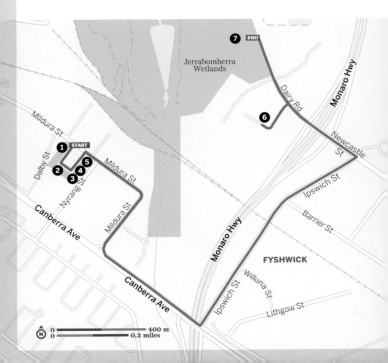

❶ Fyshwick Fresh Food Markets

One of Fyshwick's main drawcards is its produce market (p121), which first opened in 1965 and has been going strong ever since. Feast your eyes on seasonal fruits and vegetables in every colour imaginable; it's a haven for self-caterers.

❷ Deli Planet

In the centre of the markets, this amazing Italian **deli** (☏02-6295 8067; www.deliplanet.net.au; Fyshwick Fresh Food Markets, 12 Dalby St, ⏰8am-5.30pm Thu-Sun) sells gourmet goods galore, from cheeses and charcuterie to jams, sauces and dips. It's a fabulous place to stock up on picnic supplies.

❸ Krofne

Opened in 2017, Fyshwick's Niche Markets offer an ever-expanding array of stalls. Named after the Croatian word for doughnut, **Krofne** (☏0409 846 906; www.facebook.com/krofnecbr; Niche Markets, 36 Mildura St; doughnuts from $4.50; ⏰10am-5pm Thu & Fri, from 9am Sat & Sun) dishes out delicious doughnuts with a range of fillings, from Nutella to rose-hip jam. The stall provides employment opportunities for young people with disabilities.

❹ Piccolo Market Coffee

Fuel your shopping with a smooth takeaway espresso from **Piccolo Market Coffee** (www.facebook.com/piccolomrktcoffee; Niche Markets, 36 Mildura St; ⏰7.30am-4pm Thu-Sun), run by the Caputo family, who have been kicking around the Canberra hospitality industry for over 15 years.

❺ Urban Thyme

We can't resist the *manouche* (Lebanese-style pizza topped with zaatar spice) at this lovely little **bakery** (www.facebook.com/urban-thymecanberra; Niche Markets, 36 Mildura St; dishes from $7; ⏰7.30am-4.30pm Thu-Sun). The smiling staff will talk you through the options and give your chosen dish a squeeze of lemon before packaging it up for you to take home.

❻ Capital Brewing Co

Once you've finished at the market, it's a fairly dull 3km walk to your next destination, but the end point makes it worthwhile. Pull up a pew at **Capital Brewing Co** (☏02-5104 0915; www.capitalbrewing.co; Bldg 3, 1 Dairy Rd; ⏰11.30am-late) and taste its locally brewed ales and lagers straight from the tap.

❼ Jerrabomberra Wetlands

Work off all the food and drink you've consumed at the **Jerrabomberra Wetlands** (www.jerrabomberrawetlands.org.au; Dairy Rd), a nature reserve in Fyshwick's northern reaches that's home to more than 200 species of birds as well as turtles, frogs and platypuses. There are plenty of marked trails throughout the wetlands to help you explore this unique ecosystem.

Worth a Trip 🔭
Tidbinbilla Nature Reserve

Less than an hour's drive from Canberra, this nature park is a key habitat for some of Australia's best-known animals: kangaroos, koalas and emus. A predator-protected sanctuary is your best chance to spot these critters in the wild. The breeding program at the park also includes the rare brush-tailed rock wallaby and the colourful corroboree tree frog.

📞 02-6205 1233

www.tidbinbilla.act.gov.au

141 Paddys River Rd, Paddys River

entry per car $13

🕑 7.30am-6pm Apr-Nov, to 8pm Oct-Mar, visitor centre 9am-5pm

Visitor Centre

The entry point to Tidbinbilla, stop here to pay your entry fee and get tips from the rangers about self-guided walks, tours and other activities taking place in the park during your visit.

Sanctuary

This wetlands ecosystem is surrounded by bushland and skirted by a predator-proof fence, making it a perfect refuge for all kinds of native animals. Walking tracks abound: as well as the ever-popular Koala Path, you can walk the 90-minute (2.1km) boardwalk loop past ponds and bushland where lucky visitors might spot wallabies, echidnas and the elusive platypus. A separate hour-long (1.6km) path departs from the Black Flats car park.

Koala Path

A 20-minute, well-graded walk takes in the koala enclosure, where you're basically guaranteed to get a glimpse of these furry crowd favourites, as well as 700m of koala habitat. You might also spot wombats, wallabies and echidnas.

Walking Trails

There are 23 different marked walking trails scattered throughout Tidbinbilla, from short 500m strolls to an all-day, 19km hike. Staff at the visitor centre can advise on current conditions and recommend trails based on your needs and level of fitness. Don't forget to pack sufficient water and sun protection.

Nature Discovery Playground

A little way into the park you'll encounter this excellent adventure playground set among a variety of different picnic spots, some with communal barbecues and picnic tables. Kids will love scrambling over the farm-themed equipment.

★ Top Tips

o Free guided tours take place throughout the day, ranging from 45-minute introductory talks to two-hour exploratory meanders. Check at the visitor centre to see what's going on.

o If you have a particular interest – koalas, perhaps, or corroboree tree frogs – check online for specialised up-close-and-personal sessions that run occasionally during the year.

✕ Take a Break

There's a small cafe in the visitor centre selling coffee, ice creams, snacks and other basic refreshments, but your best bet is to bring your own picnic and make the most of the numerous scenic picnic areas scattered throughout the park.

★ Getting There

🚌 You'll need your own wheels to get to (and around) Tidbinbilla. It's a 45-minute drive from central Canberra.

Worth a Trip 👀
Namadgi National Park

The name Namadgi comes from the Ngunnawal word for the mountains southwest of Canberra, and this national park includes eight of those peaks higher than 1700m. Walking opportunities abound throughout the park, from short hour-long strolls to multiday hiking adventures. There are also opportunities for mountain biking, fishing and horse riding, along with the chance to view Aboriginal rock art.

📞 02-6207 2900

www.environment.act.
gov.au

Naas Rd, Tharwa

admission free

🕐 visitor centre 9am-4pm

Visitor Centre

Located at the main entry point to the national park, 2km south of Tharwa, staff at this friendly visitor centre can advise on hiking and mountain-biking trails, and dispense maps and brochures. If you're headed out on a hike, be sure to stop here on the way through for an update on the latest conditions.

Booroomba Rocks

A steep, 2.5km (1½-hour) return walking track leads to these amazing granite cliffs, which offer jaw-dropping views of the surrounding mountains. You'll puff a bit on the way up, but the reward is definitely worth it. Note that the road to Booroomba car park, the beginning of the walk, is steep and may be impassable to smaller 2WD vehicles during wet weather.

Yankee Hat

This 6km (2½-hour) walk through grasslands brings you to the Yankee Hat Shelter, an indigenous rock-art site at least 800 years old (though Indigenous Australians were present in the area up to 3700 years ago). Images of dingoes, turtles and kangaroos feature in the paintings, as well as human figures. Do not touch the rock art: oil from your skin can damage the paintings. The walk departs from the car park at the end of Old Boboyan Rd – pick up a map at the visitor centre on your way past.

Snow!

If you're here during the dry summer months this may seem unlikely, but Namadgi frequently receives a sprinkling of snow come winter. When the white stuff is around, the area at the top of Mount Franklin Rd is the best spot to get in on the tobogganing and snow-play action: check with the visitor centre before you head up to make sure the road is open.

★ Top Tips

○ Camping is possible at three campsites within the park: Honeysuckle, Mt Clear and Orroral. Book online or at the visitor centre (per person $6 to $10).

○ On total fire ban days sections of the park may be closed due to safety concerns; check with the visitor centre before setting out.

✖ Take a Break

There are no shops or cafes within the park, but picnic areas abound. Be sure to bring supplies to last your entire visit, including water.

The small **general store** (☎ 02-6237 5142; 11 North St, Tharwa; ⊙ 9am-5.30pm) sells coffee, cold drinks, pies and ice creams.

★ Getting There

🚗 You'll need your own wheels to access the vast Namadgi National Park. The visitor's centre is a 40-minute drive from Canberra.

Worth a Trip 🔭
Canberra Wine Region

Canberra's cool winters and long summers make the city's northern region a perfect spot for growing cool-climate vines such as pinot noir and riesling. Viticulturists first began dabbling here more than 160 years ago, and the 1970s saw the industry begin to boom. Nowadays there are more than 30 wineries tucked around the hills only a half-hour drive from the city centre.

Getting There

🚗 Most wineries are 20km to 30km from Canberra, near Murrumbateman and Hall. There is no public transport out here – if you don't have your own vehicle, your best bet is to join a guided tour.

Clonakilla Wines

One of the ACT's earliest wine producers, **Clonakilla Wines** (☏02-6227 5877; www.clonakilla. com.au; 3 Crisps Lane, Murrumbateman; ⊙11am-4pm Mon-Fri, 10am-5pm Sat & Sun) was founded by CSIRO scientist John Kirk in 1971. The winery makes a handful of highly sought-after drops, including some of the country's best shiraz viognier. Taste them all at the lovely stone cellar door, where you can also purchase small cheese platters to accompany your favourite drop.

Eden Road Wines

The (relatively) new-kid-on-the-block of the Canberra wine scene, **Eden Road Wines** (☏02-6226 8800; www.edenroadwines.com.au; 3182 Barton Hwy, Murrumbateman; ⊙11am-4.30pm Wed-Sun) has been producing fantastic, award-winning shiraz since 2008. Many of its vineyards are on-site; however, it also has vines in Gundagai and Tumbarumba. Taste some of the fruits of its labour at the friendly cellar door, where you can also order a cheese platter ($20) if you're feeling peckish.

Helm Wines

Some of the region's best riesling can be sampled at **Helm Wines** (☏02-6227 5953; www. helmwines.com.au; 19 Butts Rd, Murrumbateman; ⊙10am-5pm Thu-Mon). The pretty tasting room is a former schoolhouse built in 1888. If you're lucky, Ken Helm himself might be on-site to guide you through the tasting and dispense some of his boundless knowledge about the industry.

Poachers Pantry

This **restaurant** (☏02-6230 2487; www.poachers pantry.com.au; 431 Nanima Rd, Springrange; mains breakfast $18-22, lunch $31-43, platters $18-36;

★ **Top Tips**

o Many cellar doors close on Mondays and Tuesdays, so try to avoid visiting the region on those days.

o A wide range of companies offer guided winery tours, from basic minibus tours to luxury limousine rides. The visitor centre (p142) can advise on the best tour for your budget, or visit www.canberrawines. com.au.

✕ **Take a Break**

If you've got vineyard fatigue, stop in at the small village of Hall for a stroll and maybe some coffee and cake – we like Kynefin (p111).

11.30am-3pm Mon-Fri, from 9.30am Sat & Sun) at Wily Trout Vineyard is renowned for its smoked meats and fish, but there are plenty of other options, including excellent cheese boards and tasty desserts. From Monday to Wednesday the kitchen only serves platters – but this isn't really a downside, because a platter and a glass of local wine on the deck overlooking the gardens is a truly lovely thing. There's also a small on-site **cellar door & farm shop** (02-6230 2487; www. wilytrout.com.au; 431 Nanima Rd, Springrange; 9.30am-5pm).

Shaw Vineyard Estate

A swish new cellar door with expansive views over the surrounding vines makes the tasting experience at **Shaw Vineyard Estate** (02-6227 5827; www.shawwines. com.au; 34 Isabel Dr, Murrumbateman; 10am-5pm) a cut above. Tastings are a sit-down affair, with a small charge ($5) redeemable against any purchase. Its award-winning cabernet sauvignon is a winner with us, too.

Brindabella Hills Winery

A distance away from the main Murrumbateman wine region, the sizeable **Brindabella Hills Winery** (02-6161 9154; www.brindabellahills.

Canberra District Wine Week

If you're in town in April, be sure to check out Canberra District Wine Week – the 'week' stretches for 10 days and features wine tastings, special dining events and tours at wineries all around the Canberra region.

com.au; 156 Woodgrove Cl, Wallaroo; 10am-5pm Sat & Sun) has been operating from a beautiful ridge near Hall, 26km northwest of central Canberra, for 30 years. It has won awards for its chardonnay and shiraz, which can all be tasted at the friendly cellar door. There's also a lovely cafe.

Four Winds Vineyard

Family-owned and run **Four Winds Vineyard** (02-6227 0189; www.fourwindsvineyard.com.au; 9 Patemans Lane, Murrumbateman; 10am-4pm Thu-Mon) is popular with locals, who love to book a table on weekends and linger over a glass of their favourite drop while devouring wood-fired pizzas ($17). Interesting wines – including a sparkling riesling and a cabernet rosé – make for a great tasting experience, too.

Survival Guide

Glebe Park (p80) SLOW WALKER/SHUTTERSTOCK ©

Before You Go

Book Your Stay

o Canberra has a wide range of accommodation, though much of it is in the mid- to high-range bracket due to the constant influx of politicians and public servants.

o Accommodation is most expensive on parliamentary sitting days. See www.aph.gov.au/about_parliament/sitting_calendar to check whether parliament will be sitting during your visit.

o Hotels charge peak rates midweek, but often have reduced rates at weekends.

o Peak rates also apply during the spring Floriade festival.

o Book well ahead – and usually via the hotel's website – for the best deals.

Useful Websites

Visit Canberra (www.visitcanberra.com.au/accommodation) Find

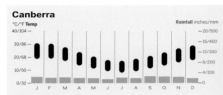

Canberra

When to Go

o **Spring** The city blooms with colour during the Floriade festival in September and October.

o **Summer** Late autumn to early summer (November to December) is a great time to visit, with pleasant daytime temperatures and long sunlight hours.

o **Autumn** The city is its most picturesque in mid-March, when hot-air balloons fill the sky during the Canberra Balloon Spectacular.

o **Winter** Canberra's winters can be bitterly cold. Warm-blooded types should avoid June to August, though this is a great time to visit the museums.

out about the newest developments in hotels and accommodation on Canberra's official tourism website.

Lonely Planet (lonelyplanet.com/australia/australian-capital-territory/canberra/hotels) Recommendations and bookings.

Best Budget

Little National Hotel (www.littlenationalhotel.com.au) Overlooking parliament, this slick hotel has petite

but well-designed rooms and great communal areas.

Canberra City YHA (www.yha.com.au) Central, well-organised backpackers with all the trimmings.

Blue & White Lodge (www.blueandwhitelodge.com.au) Spotless and friendly budget motel in the outer northern suburbs.

Alvio Tourist Park (www.aliviogroup.com.au) Spot kangaroos and other wildlife at this well-equipped bushland caravan park.

Best Midrange

East Hotel (www.east hotel.com.au) Studio rooms, clever design and three excellent dining options make this hotel a cut above.

University House (www.unihouse.anu. edu.au) This grand dame is peacefully secluded inside the ANU campus but still within easy reach of the city.

Hotel Realm (www. hotelrealm.com. au) A classy design hotel with exceptionally comfy beds and great advance-booking perks.

Peppers Gallery Hotel (www.peppers.com. au/gallery) Within the hip New Acton precinct, this friendly hotel is cool by association.

Vibe Canberra Airport (www.vibehotels.com/ hotel/canberra-airport) Chic hotel within handy walking distance from the airport terminal.

Mantra MacArthur Hotel (www.mantra hotels.com/mantra -macarthur-hotel) A spic and span business

Top Tip

Everything from accommodation to dinner reservations gets busier in Canberra during parliamentary sitting weeks; consider visiting during off weeks or on the weekend.

hotel with studio rooms, located just off North-bourne Ave.

Best Top End

Ovolo Nishi (www. ovolohotels.com.au/ ovolonishi) A genuine art hotel, with delightful design touches around every corner, in a hip cultural precinct.

Hyatt Hotel Canberra (www.hyatt. com) Canberra's most historic hotel, popular with visiting dignitaries and the like.

Burbury Hotel (www. burburyhotel.com.au) A business hotel with luxe suites and a handy Barton location.

Arriving in Canberra

Most travellers will arrive in Canberra by air or by road. Canberra airport has

several daily flights to most Australian capital cities, as well as regular international flights to Singapore and Doha (sometimes with a brief stopover in Sydney). By road, Canberra is three hours from Sydney and seven hours from Melbourne. There are also three daily trains to/from Sydney (four hours) and one train/ bus combination to Melbourne (nine hours).

Flights, cars and tours can be booked online at lonelyplanet. com/bookings.

Canberra Airport

The **airport** (☎ 02-6275 2222; www.canberra airport.com.au; Terminal Ave, Pialligo) is located within the city itself, only 7km southeast of Civic.

Daily domestic flights service most Australian capital

cities and some regional destinations.

o Qantas (www.qantas.com) flies to/from Adelaide, Brisbane, Melbourne, Perth and Sydney.

o Virgin Australia (www.virginaustralia.com.au) flies to/from Adelaide, Brisbane, Gold Coast, Melbourne and Sydney.

o Tigerair Australia (www.tigerair.com.au) also heads to Melbourne.

o FlyPelican (www.flypelican.com.au) serves Newcastle and Dubbo.

Only a few international destinations are available, with most international travellers transiting through Sydney.

o Singapore Airlines (www.singaporeair.com), flies daily to/from Singapore (with a brief stop in Sydney inbound).

o Qatar Airways (www.qatarairways.com) flies daily to/from Doha also with a brief stop in Sydney.

From the airport, a taxi to the city centre costs from $30 to $40. Buses run regularly into the city between 6am and 6pm (adult/

child $5/2.50, 20 to 40 minutes).

Jolimont Centre

The interstate bus terminal is in the centre of Civic at the **Jolimont Centre** (Map p76, F5; 67 Northbourne Ave, Civic; ⏱5am-10.30pm), where you'll find booking desks for the major bus companies.

Greyhound Australia (☑ 02-6211 8545; www.greyhound.com.au; 65 Northbourne Ave) has daily coaches to Sydney (from $39, 3½ hours), Albury (from $62, 4½ hours) and Melbourne (from $69, eight hours), along with seasonal buses to the ski resorts.

Murrays (☑ 13 22 51; www.murrays.com.au; 65 Northbourne Ave; ⏱3.30am-6pm) offers express services to Sydney (from $39, 3½ hours), Wollongong ($49, 3¼ hours), Batemans Bay ($38, 2½ hours), Moruya ($41, 3¼ hours) and Narooma ($49, 4½ hours), as well as the ski fields.

NSW TrainLink's (☑ 13 22 32; www.nswtrainlink.info) coaches depart

Canberra Railway Station on the Canberra–Cooma–Merimbula–Eden (daily) and Canberra–Cooma–Jindabyne (three per week) routes.

Canberra Railway Station

NSW TrainLink (☑ 13 22 32; www.nswtrainlink.info) operates Services from Sydney ($28, 4¼ hours), Bowral ($17, 2½ hours), Bundanoon ($15, two hours) and Bungendore ($3.50, 40 minutes) pull into Kingston's **Canberra Railway Station** (☑ 13 22 32; Burke Cres, Kingston) three times daily.

V/Line (☑ 1800 800 007; www.vline.com.au) offers a daily service combines a train from Melbourne to Wodonga with a bus to Canberra (from $67, nine hours), terminating at the Jolimont Centre.

Arriving by Car

The Hume Hwy connects Sydney and Melbourne, passing 50km north of Canberra. The Federal Hwy runs north to connect with the Hume near Goulburn, and the Barton Hwy (Rte 25) meets the Hume near Yass. To the south, the Monaro Hwy connects Canberra with Cooma.

Minimum journey times to/from Canberra include the following:

Sydney (290km, three hours)

Melbourne (670km, seven hours)

Wollongong (250km, 2½ hours)

Batemans Bay (150km, two hours)

Getting Around

Bicycle

○ Canberra has an extensive network of on-road bicycle lanes and off-road cycling routes, making two wheels an excellent option for getting around the city. Note that wearing a helmet while cycling is mandatory in Australia.

○ Many hotels and accommodation providers offer bicycle hire for guests. Other options include the following:

Share a Bike (1300 588 533; www.shareabike.com.au; per 1/4/24hr $12/24/36) has seven stations scattered across the city outside various hotels; hotel reception can provide locks and helmets (included in the price).

Cycle Canberra (0449 557 838; www.cyclecanberra.com.au/bikehirecanberra; per day from $50; delivery 8-11am Mon-Sat) will deliver bikes to your hotel for free with advance reservation. Also offers a 'family rate' (two adults and two kids per day $105).

Bus

○ The bus network, operated by **Transport Canberra** (13 17 10; www.transport.act.gov.au; single adult/child $5/2.50, day pass $9.60/4.80), will get you to most places of interest in the city. A useful journey planner is available on the website.

○ Travellers can use the MyWay smart-card system, but if you're only here for a week or so you're better off paying the driver in cash, as a card costs a nonrefundable fee of adult/child $5/2.50. A day pass costs less than two single tickets, so purchase one on your first journey of the day.

○ What is referred to as the city bus interchange is actually a set of 11 bus stops scattered along Northbourne Ave, Alinga St, East Row and Mort St.

Light Rail

○ Canberra's new light-rail line from Civic to Gungahlin via Dickson commenced services in 2019.

○ The 12km route has 13 stops, including several along Northbourne Ave that are of use to travellers visiting Braddon and Dickson.

○ The existing bus ticketing system has been expanded to cover the light-rail line, with passengers able to purchase tickets from vending machines at the light-rail stops before boarding.

○ Check the Transport Canberra website for more information.

Car & Motorcycle

o Canberra's road system is as circuitous as a politician's answer to a straight question. That said, the wide and relatively uncluttered streets make driving easy, even during Canberra's so-called 'peak hour'.

o There is plenty of paid parking around major tourist sights and in the city centre, and most hotels also offer parking, often for an additional charge.

Taxi

Cabxpress (02-6181 2700; www.cabxpress. com.au)

Canberra Elite Taxis (02-6126 1600; www. canberraelite.com.au)

Essential Information

Accessible Travel

o In general, Canberra's hotels, shops and restaurants are very accessible to travellers with disabilities or mobility issues.

o Canberra's top sights, including Parliament House (p34), the National Gallery of Australia (p40), the National Portrait Gallery (p50) and Questacon (p44) are all accessible to wheelchair users and have a variety of accommodations for visually

and hearing-impaired visitors.

o The website www. getaboutable.com is a Canberra-based initiative that uses crowd-sourced contributions to review the accessibility of businesses around the world, with a large amount of information about Canberra and its surrounds.

o Over 80% of Canberra's buses and bus stops are accessible for wheelchair users, with Transport Canberra committed to a goal of 100% accessibility by 2022. See www. transport.act.gov.au/ about-us/accessible-travel for up-to-date information.

Business Hours

Canberra doesn't have a high season as such, but some restaurants in Parkes and Barton may have longer hours during parliamentary sitting weeks.

Banks 9.30am to 4pm or 5pm Monday to Friday

Bars 5pm to midnight Sunday to Thursday, to 2am Friday and Saturday

Cafes 8am to 4pm

Nightclubs 8pm to 3am or 4am Thursday to Sunday

Restaurants noon to 2.30pm and 6pm to 10pm, often closed Monday

Shops 10am to 5pm

Electricity

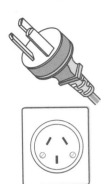

Type I
230V/50Hz

Emergencies

In an emergency dial
📞000 to reach the
police, fire and ambu-
lance services.

Insurance

A travel-insurance poli-
cy to cover theft, loss
and medical problems
is a very good idea.

Level of Cover Ensure
your policy covers
theft, loss and medical
problems. Some poli-
cies specifically exclude
designated 'dangerous
activities' such as scuba
diving, skiing and even
bushwalking. Make sure
the policy you choose
fully covers your

planned (and perhaps
unplanned) activities.

Health Check that the
policy covers ambu-
lances and emergency
medical evacuations
by air. Australia is a
vast country so being
airlifted to a hospital is
a real possibility.

Worldwide travel
insurance is available
at www.lonelyplanet.
com/travel-insurance.
You can buy, extend
and claim online any-
time – even if you're
already on the road.

Internet Access

A free public wifi
network known as
CBRfree is available in
the Canberra central
business district and
across many public
areas throughout the
city, though service
can sometimes be
patchy.

Most hotels and
many businesses
also provide wifi for
patrons.

Legal Matters

Most travellers will
have zero contact with
Australia's police or
legal system; if they
do, it's most likely to
be while driving.

Driving There's a significant police presence
on Australian roads,
and police have the
power to stop your car,
see your licence (you're
required to carry it),
check your vehicle for
road-worthiness and
insist that you take a
breath test for alcohol
(and sometimes illicit
drugs).

Drugs First-time of-
fenders caught with
small amounts of
illegal drugs are likely
to receive a fine rather
than go to jail, but the
recording of a convic-
tion against you may
affect your visa status.

Visas If you remain in
Australia beyond the
life of your visa, you'll
officially be an 'over-
stayer' and could face
mandatory detention
and be prevented from
returning to Australia.

Legal advice It's your
right to telephone
a lawyer or relative
before police question-
ing begins. Legal aid
is available in serious
cases and is subject
to means testing; for
legal aid info see www.
nationallegalaid.org.
However, many solici-
tors do not charge for
an initial consultation.

LGBT+ Travellers

o LGBTIQ+ travellers shouldn't encounter any problems in Canberra, with liberal attitudes generally prevailing.

o Canberra's most well-known gay club is Cube (p86); check the website for upcoming events.

o In November Canberra hosts SpringOUT, a month-long pride festival featuring a wide variety of events and activities. See www.springout.com.au for more information.

o **Diversity ACT** (☎02-6231 3126; www.diversityact.org.au; 8 Laidlaw Pl, Kambah; ⏰10am-2pm Tue, 5-8pm Wed, 2-6pm Thu, noon-4pm Sat) Operates a drop-in hub that offers a safe space for LGBTIQ+ people.

Media

o **Newspapers** The daily national broadsheet *The Australian* is complemented by local newspapers in every major city and many regional towns.

o **Radio** ABC broadcasts national radio programs, many syndicated from the BBC, plus local regional stations. Check www.abc.net.au/radio for local frequencies.

o **Television** The main free-to-air TV channels are the ABC, multi-cultural SBS, Seven, Nine and Ten. Though locals are being seduced by paid TV options like Foxtel and Netflix.

Money

ATMs (cashpoints) are easy to find and most accept international cards. Most businesses – even, increasingly, market-stall holders – accept payment by card.

Dos & Don'ts

There are very few rules of etiquette to take into account in Australia.

o **Greetings** Usually a simple 'G'day', smile or nod suffices when passing people. Shake hands with men or women when meeting for the first time. Australians expect a firm handshake with eye contact.

o **Aboriginal Communities** Direct eye contact can be considered overbearing. Be respectful, wait to be acknowledged and respond in a like manner.

o **Dry Communities** Check whether alcohol restrictions apply when visiting remote communities. You may be breaking the law if you have booze in your vehicle.

o **BBQs** Bring your own drinks, and some sausages (aka 'snags') if invited to a BBQ.

o **Photography** Ask before taking pictures of people. Particularly bear in mind that for Aboriginal Australians, photography can be highly intrusive, and photographing cultural places, practices and images, sites of significance and ceremonies may not be welcomed. Respect is essential.

ATMs

ATMs Australia's 'big four' banks – ANZ, Commonwealth, National Australia Bank and Westpac – and affiliated banks have branches all over Australia, plus a slew of 24-hour cashpoints (automated teller machines; ATMs). You'll even find them in some outback roadhouses.

Eftpos Most petrol stations, supermarkets, restaurants, cafes and shops have Electronic Funds Transfer at Point of Sale (Eftpos) facilities.

Bank fees Withdrawing cash through ATMs or Eftpos may attract significant fees – check associated costs with your home bank and enquire about fee-free options.

Credit Cards

Credit cards are widely accepted for everything from a hostel bed or a restaurant meal to an adventure tour, and are essential for hiring a car. They can also be used to get cash advances over the counter at banks and from many ATMs, depending on the card, though you'll incur immediate interest. Diners Club and American Express (Amex) are not as widely accepted in Australia.

Currency

Australia's currency is the Australian dollar, comprising 100 cents. There are 5c, 10c, 20c, 50c, $1 and $2 coins, and $5, $10, $20, $50 and $100 notes. Prices in shops are often marked in single cents then rounded to the nearest 5c when you pay.

Debit Cards

A debit card allows you to draw money directly from your home bank account. Any card connected to the international banking network – Cirrus, Maestro, Plus and Eurocard – should work with your PIN, but again expect substantial fees. Companies such as Travelex offer debit cards with set withdrawal fees and a balance you can top up from your personal bank account while on the road.

Surcharge

Many hospitality businesses charge a 10% to 15% surcharge on Sundays and public holidays to cover increased wage costs; this will usually be noted on the bottom of your menu and is non-negotiable.

Tipping

Tipping is rarely necessary, though some high-end places will add a 10% to 15% service charge to your bill. Many bars and cafes have a 'tip jar' for loose change.

Public Holidays

Public holidays in the ACT include the following:

New Year's Day
1 January

Australia Day
26 January, or next weekday if this falls on a weekend

Canberra Day Second Monday in March

Good Friday March or April

Easter Saturday March or April

Easter Sunday March or April

Easter Monday March or April

Anzac Day 25 April, or next weekday if this falls on a weekend

Reconciliation Day First Monday after 27 May

Queen's Birthday Second Monday in June

Labour Day First Monday in October

Christmas Day 25 December

Boxing Day 26 December

Safe Travel

Canberra is a safe city, with very low incidences of violent crime. Beyond the usual precautions you would take when visiting any major city, there's little you need to do to guarantee your personal safety.

Canberra City Police Station (☏ 02-6256 7777; www.police.act.gov. au; 16-18 London Circuit, Civic)

Telephone

Either set up global roaming or pick up a local rechargeable SIM card on arrival – most supermarkets and convenience stores sell SIM cards. Popular networks include Telstra, Optus and Vodafone.

Toilets

o Toilets in Australia are sit-down Western style (though you mightn't find this prospect too appealing in some remote pit stops).

o Most public toilets are free of charge and reasonably well looked after.

o See www.toiletmap. gov.au for public toilet locations, including disabled-access toilets.

Tourist Information

Canberra & Region Visitors Centre (Map p76, B5; ☏ 02-6205 0044; www.visitcanberra.com. au; Regatta Point, Barrine Dr, Commonwealth Park; ⊙9am-5pm Mon-Fri, to 4pm Sat & Sun) Staff at this exceptionally helpful centre can dispense masses of information and brochures, including the free quarterly *Canberra Events* brochure.

Also rents out collapsible bikes (per two hours/day adult $20/45, child $15/30).

Visas

All international visitors except New Zealanders require visas to enter Australia. There are several different visas available from short-stay visitor visas to working-holiday visas.

Behind the Scenes

Send Us Your Feedback

We love to hear from travellers – your comments help make our books better. We read every word, and we guarantee that your feedback goes straight to the authors. Visit **lonelyplanet.com/contact** to submit your updates and suggestions.

Note: We may edit, reproduce and incorporate your comments in Lonely Planet products such as guidebooks, websites and digital products, so let us know if you don't want your comments reproduced or your name acknowledged. For a copy of our privacy policy visit lonelyplanet.com/privacy.

Samantha's Thanks

My thanks to Canberra locals Rachel, Sam, Emma, Harry and Lily for sharing all your insider tips. Thanks also to my travelling companions Karyn, Bill and Gemma for helping me cram as many meals into each day as possible. Lastly, thanks to everyone at Lonely Planet for their hard work on this title, and especially to Tasmin Waby for once again throwing me in the deep end with complete faith in my swimming abilities.

Acknowledgements

Cover photograph: Australian Parliament House, designed by architect Romaldo Giurgola; Forecourt Mosaic Pavement (1986–87) by Michael Nelson Jagamara (born 1945) Luritja/Warlpiri peoples. Image by Andrew Watson, AWL Images©

This Book

This 1st edition of Lonely Planet's *Pocket Canberra* was researched and written by Samantha Forge. This guidebook was produced by the following:

Destination Editor
Tasmin Waby

Senior Product Editors
Kate Chapman, Anne Mason

Regional Senior Cartographer
Julie Sheridan

Product Editor
Katie Connolly

Book Designer
Brooke Giacomin

Assisting Editors Kellie Langdon, Kristin Odijk, Gabrielle Stefanos

Cover Researcher
Naomi Parker

Thanks to Carolyn Boicos, Andi Jones, Virginia Moreno, Susan Paterson, Kathryn Rowan, Vicky Smith, Angela Tinson

Index

See also separate subindexes for:

❸ **Eating** p147

❸ **Drinking** p147

❸ **Entertainment** p148

❸ **Shopping** p148